The Loyalists
of
Pennsylvania

By
Wilbur H. Siebert

Souther Historical Press, Inc,
Greenville, South Carolina

Please direct all correspondence and book orders to:
SOUTHERN HISTORICAL PRESS, Inc.
PO Box 1267
Greenville, SC   29602-1267

Originally published 1920 by:
    The Ohio State University Bulletin, volume XXIV
ISBN #978-1-63914-230-9
Printed in the United States of America

CONTENTS

CHAPTER I

THE LOYALISTS ON THE UPPER OHIO

CHAPTER II

THE LOYALISTS OF NORTHEASTERN PENNSYLVANIA

✕ CHAPTER III

THE REPRESSION OF LOYALISTS AND NEUTRALS IN SOUTHEASTERN PENNSYLVANIA

CHAPTER IV

THE BRITISH INVASION OF SOUTHEASTERN PENNSYLVANIA, AUGUST 25, 1777, to JUNE 18, 1778

CHAPTER V

WHIG REPRISALS UPON LOYALISTS DURING AND AFTER THE BRITISH OCCUPATION OF PHILADELPHIA

CHAPTER VI

THE PURCHASE OF THE INDIAN TRACT ON LAKE ERIE

CHAPTER VII

THE SURVIVAL OF LOYALISM AFTER THE DEPARTURE OF THE BRITISH FROM THE STATE

CHAPTER VIII

THE PARDON OF ATTAINTED LOYALISTS BY THE SUPREME EXECUTIVE COUNCIL, 1780-1790

CHAPTER IX

THE SALE OF FORFEITED ESTATES

CHAPTER X

THE EMIGRATION OF PENNSYLVANIA LOYALISTS

BIBLIOGRAPHY

DIARIES, LETTERS, AND PERSONAL NARRATIVES

"Bethlehem During the Revolution. Extracts from the Diaries in the Moravian Archives at Bethlehem, Pa." In *The Pennsylvania Magazine of History and Biography*, XII, No. 4.

Calendar of the Correspondence of George Washington, I.

Dexter, F. B., ed.: *The Literary Diary of Ezra Stiles, D.D., LL.D.*, 1776-1795. Three vols.

"Diary of James Allen, Esq., of Philadelphia, Counsellor-at-Law, 1770-1778." In *The Pennsylvania Magazine of History and Biography*, IX, Nos. 2, 3, 4.

Diary and Letters of His Excellency, Thomas Hutchinson, II.

"Diary of Robert Morton." In *The Pennsylvania Magazine*, I.

Duane, William, ed.: *Extracts from the Diary of Christopher Marshall . . . 1774-1781*. Passages from the Diary of Christopher Marshall, kept in Philadelphia and Lancaster during the American Revolution, I, 1774-1777. (Phila., Dec., 1849.)

"Extracts form the Journal of Mrs. Henry Drinker, of Philadelphia, from September 25, 1777, to July 4, 1778." In *The Pennsylvania Magazine of History and Biography*, XIII, No. 3.

Gilpin, Thomas, ed.: *Exiles in Virginia: with Observations on the Conduct of the Society of Friends during the Revolutionary War, comprising the Offical Papers of the Government relating to that Period. 1777-1778*. (Phila., 1848.)

Journal and Letters of the late Samuel Curwen, Judge of Admiralty, etc., a Loyalist Refugee in England, during the American Revolution. 3d ed.

"Letters of Robert Proud." In *The Pennsylvania Magazine of History and Biography*, XXXIV, No. 133.

"Letters of Thomas Wharton, 1773-1783." In *The Pennsylvania Magazine of History and Biography*, XXXIV, No. 133.

"Narrative of the Transactions, Imprisonment and Sufferings of John Connolly, an American Loyalist and Lieutenant-Colonel in His Majesty's Service." In *The Pennsylvania Magazine of History and Biography*, XII, Nos. 3 and 4; XIII, No. 3.

"Narrative or Journal of Capt. John Ferdinand Dalziel Smyth, of the Queen's Rangers." In *The Pennsylvania Magazine of History and Biography*, XXXIX, No. 154.

Narrative of James Moody.

"Popp's Journal, 1777-1783." In *The Pennsylvania Magazine of History and Biography*, XXVI, No. 101.

Raymond, Rev. W. O., ed.: *Winslow Papers, A.D. 1776-1826*.

Thwaites, R. G., and Kellogg, Louise P., *Frontier Defense on the Upper Ohio*.

BIOGRAPHIES

Baldwin, Ernest H., "Joseph Galloway, the Loyalist Politician." In *The Pennsylvania Magazine of History and Biography*, XXVI, Nos. 102, 103, 104.

Burton, C. M., "John Connolly, a Tory of the Revolution." In the *Proceedings* of the American Antiquarian Society, Oct., 1909.

Read, D. B., *Life and Times of Governor Simcoe*.

Sabine, Lorenzo, *Biographical Sketches of Loyalists of the American Revolution*. Two vols.

Scott, Duncan C., *John Graves Simcoe*.

STATE AND LOCAL HISTORIES

"The Penfield Records." In *Collections of the New Brunswick Historical Society*, No. 4.

Haliburton, Thomas C., *History of Nova Scotia*, II.

Ganong, W. F., *Monograph of Historic Sites in the Province of New Brunswick; Monograph of the Origins of the Settlements in New Brunswick*.

Jack, D. R., *Centennial Prize Essay on the History of the City and County of St. John, N. B.*

Papers read before the Lancaster County Historical Society, XII, No. 6.

Proud, Robert, *The History of Pennsylvania . . . Of the General State in which it Flourished, principally between the Years 1760 and 1770. Written principally between the Years 1776 and 1780*.

Raymond, Rev. W. O., "Early Days of Woodstock, N. B." In *The Dispatch* of Woodstock, N. B., December, 1906, and January, 1907.

Raymond, Rev. W. O., *The River St. John*.

Scharf, *History of Maryland.*

Vroom, J., *Courier Series,* LXXII.

Scharf and Westcott, *History of Philadelphia,* I.

Siebert, Wilbur H., "The Loyalists in West Florida and the Natchez District." In *The Mississippi Valley Historical Review,* II, March, 1916; "The Loyalists and Six Nation Indians in the Niagara Peninsula." In *Transactions of the Royal Society of Canada,* IX. "Refugee Loyalists of Connecticut." In *Transactions of the Royal Society of Canada,* Series III, Volume X. "The Tories of the Upper Ohio." In *Biennial Report,* Archives and History, West Virginia, 1911-1914.

Stryker, William S., *The New Jersey Volunteers (Loyalists) in the Revolutionary War.* (Pamphlet.)

OFFICIAL RECORDS AND LAWS

American Archives, 4th Series, IV, V, VI; 5th Series, I, II, III.

Charters, Statutes, and By-Laws of the University [of Pennsylvania]. Revised, March, 1826. (Pamphlet.)

"Claims of American Loyalists." In *The Pennsylvania Magazine of History and Biography,* XV.

Colonial Records of Pa., X, XI, XII, XIII, XIV, XV, XVI.

Examination of Joseph Galloway, Esq., Late Speaker of the House of Assembly of Pennsylvania, before the House of Commons, in a Committee on the American Papers. With Explanatory Notes. 2d ed. London, 1780.

Godfrey, Carlos E., "Muster Rolls of Three Troops of Loyalist Light Dragoons Raised in Pennsylvania, 1777-1778." In *The Pennsylvania Magazine of History and Biography,* XXXIV, No. 133.

Journal of Congress, new ed., IX.

Journals of the House of Representatives of the Commonwealth of Pennsylvania, November 28, 1776, to October, 1781-1782.

Laws of Pennsylvania, II, III.

Medical Department of the University of Pennsylvania, Oct., 1844. (Pamphlet.)

"Minutes of the Committee of Safety of Bucks County, Pa., 1774-1776." In *The Pennsylvania Magazine of History and Biography,* XV, No. 3.

Minutes of the Council of Safety of the State of New Jersey, 1777-1778. (Jersey City, 1872.)

Minutes of the Supreme Executive Council of Pennsylvania, from Its Organization to the Termination of the Revolution, March 4, 1777, to December 20, 1790. Six vols.

Report on the American Manuscripts in the Royal Institution of Great Britain, I, II, III, IV.

Second Report of the Bureau of Archives for the Province of Ontario, 1904, Parts I and II.

Statutes at Large of Pennsylvania, IX, XII, XIV.

Third Report of the Bureau of Archives for the Province of Ontario, 1905.

Winslow, Muster Master General Edward, *Muster Rolls of the* [Loyalist] *Provincial Corps.* (Unpublished.)

Griffin, *Bibliography of American Historical Societies.* 2d ed., 1907.

GENERAL AND MISCELLANEOUS WORKS

A Century of Population Growth in the United States, 1790-1900.

Drake, Francis S., *Dictionary of American Biography.*

Gentleman's Magazine, August, 1778.

Medical Department of the University of Pennsylvania. Issued by the Medical Professors of the University of Pennsylvania. (Philadelphia, October, 1844.) (Pamphlet.)

New Jersey Archives, Second Series, II, III.

Raymond, Rev. W. O., "Loyalists in Arms." In *Collections of the New Brunswick Historical Society,* No. 5.

Sargent Winthrop. ed., *Loyal Verses of Joseph Stansbury and Dr. Jonathan Odell.*

Siebert, Wilbur H., *Flight of American Loyalists to the British Isles.* (Pamphlet.) "The Dispersion of the American Tories." In *The Mississippi Valley Historical Review,* I.

CHAPTER I

THE LOYALISTS ON THE UPPER OHIO

Toryism or Loyalism became active among the frontiersmen of western Pennsylvania before it did in other parts of the Colony. This activity was evoked in the early seventeen seventies by Lord Dunmore's attempt to settle the boundary dispute between Virginia and Pennsylvania by taking forcible possession of Fort Pitt. Dunmore's agent in effecting this enterprise was Dr. John Connolly, captain commandant of the militia in the region concerned, who with about 80 of his men seized the fort at the end of January, 1774, changed its name to Fort Dunmore, organized the surrounding district into a new county, and thus supplanted or usurped the authority of Pennsylvania on the upper Ohio. The new order of things found many supporters among the old residents of Pittsburgh, those who resisted being severely dealt with by the commandant, while the neighboring Indians were subjected to depredations by Connolly and his adherents. Stirred thus to acts of retaliation, the savages were not restored to a state of submission until Dunmore had conducted the militia of the frontier counties on an expedition against them, which received the sounding appellation of Dunmore's War.

The clash of authority between the new regime and the old at Fort Dunmore is illustrated by a proclamation issued by Connolly at the end of this year. In this manifesto the commandant said that he was informed that certain persons in the region roundabout, who were called collectors, were apparently authorized to commit various deeds of violence, including the breaking open of doors, cupboards, etc., in order to extort money from the inhabitants under the name of taxes. He therefore apprised his Majesty's subjects that there could be no authority legally vested in anybody to perform such acts "at this juncture," that such measures were unwarrantable as abuses of public liberty, and that all persons had an undoubted natural, as well as lawful, right to repel them. The proclamation closed by directing the people to apprehend anyone attempting the seizure of their effects, in consequence of such

9

imaginary authority, in order that he might be dealt with according to law.[1]

In June, 1775, Connolly held an Indian council at the fort in pursuance of the programme of his patron, the governor of Virginia, to win the redmen for the King, and he tells us in his *Narrative* that he "had the happiness" of doing so. He also relates how he brought together a group of his friends—"most of them either officers in the militia, or magistrates of the county" (of West Augusta)—who entered into a secret agreement to assist in restoring constitutional government, if he could procure the necessary authority to raise men. It is clear, therefore, that Connolly and his adherents were determined to prepare for armed resistance to the revolutionary party, which had assumed control of the colonial government.

As a precautionary measure, which Dunmore deemed needful on account of the numerous friends of the American cause on the upper Ohio, the commandant disbanded the garrison of Fort Dunmore in the early days of July, and on the 20th of that month set out for Virginia to submit his plans for future operations to the official he was serving. Arrived at Norfolk, where Dunmore was already a refugee on board a British man-of-war, Connolly spent two weeks completing his arrangements, and then proceeded to Boston to lay them before General Gage. In brief, his plan was to secure the coöperation of the whites and Indians from the royal post at Detroit and the garrison from Fort Gage on the Illinois in an expedition against the upper Ohio, where he would enlist a battalion of Loyalists and some independent companies, besides gaining the active support of the neighboring Indians. With the force thus collected, he would seize or, if necessary, destroy forts Pitt and Fincastle, and form a junction with Lord Dunmore at Alexandria, thus severing the Southern Colonies from the Northern and assuring the success of the royal cause in the South. That the Indian villages might be prepared for his coming, Loyalist traders went among them to represent to them that the American "Long Knives" were no less enemies of the tribesmen than of the King. This part of Connolly's plot was the first to be thwarted, for the Committee of Correspondence of West Augusta County brought about a conference in September and October, 1775, at Pittsburgh between the tribes from the Ohio, upper Allegheny,

[1] *Colon. Records of Pa.*, X, 288.

and the neighborhood of Detroit and the commissioners of Congress, which terminated in a treaty of peace and neutrality.[2]

But other unforeseen contingencies were to arise to the complete undoing of the plot. Connolly returned to Virginia after a prolonged stay in Boston, received a commission as lieutenant colonel commandant from Dunmore, and in company with two Loyalists, Allen Cameron and Dr. John Ferdinand Dalziel Smyth, set out for Detroit, November 13. Smyth was to be appointed surgeon and Cameron a lieutenant in the battalion—the Loyal Foresters—to be raised by their companion. A week later the trio was arrested a few miles north of Hagerstown, and a few days thereafter a copy of Connolly's "proposals" was discovered in his possession, whereupon Congress was asked what should be done with the prisoners. That body ordered that they be escorted to Philadelphia under guard. On the night of December 28, Dr. Smyth escaped from the jail at Fredericktown with letters to Connolly's wife and the Tory, Alexander McKee, at Pittsburgh, as also to military officers at Kaskasia and Detroit. The latter were urged to "push down the Mississippi and join Lord Dunmore." After a perilous journey of 300 miles, the undaunted messenger was captured by a party from Fort Pitt, January 12, 1776, with Connolly's letters still on his person. He was then conveyed to Philadelphia, or as he picturesquely expresses it, he was "dragged in triumph 700 miles, bound hands and feet, to the Congress." Meantime, Connolly and Cameron had been conducted to the same destination and were brought before the Committee of Safety, January 29, but were remanded to jail to remain until further orders as persons "inimical to the liberties of America." In the following December Cameron and Smyth planned to escape from their confinement by a rope made of blankets. Smyth appears to have succeeded at this time, or soon after, for he came in with Lieutenant James Murray and 61 recruits very soon after Howe's expedition landed at the head of the Elk River, August 25, 1777, and was given a captain's commission in the Queen's Rangers a month later. In representing his own services at the close of the war, Smyth with characteristic exaggeration claimed to have raised a corps of 185 men at his own expense, in addition to others in such numbers that his recruits composed the greater part of the Rangers. Cameron, however, had the misfortune of breaking both his ankles by a fall of fifty feet, when he attempted to descend by means of the improvised rope; but he recovered sufficiently to undertake the voyage to England in the winter of 1778, the British being then in possession of Philadelphia. In the fall of 1776 Connolly was released on account of failing health, and was permitted to reside on his parole at the house of his brother-in-law, James Ewing, on the Susquehanna River. Suspicions soon arising concerning his conduct, Connolly was remanded to jail, but was again allowed to retire to Ewing's plantation, April 2, 1777, after furnishing a bond of £4,000 for his good behavior and promising not to depart more than five miles from the plantation. A little more than six months later Congress ordered its troublesome prisoner of war confined in the jail at Yorktown, where it was then sitting, on the ground that he was not acting consistently with his parole and was believed to be the prospective instrument in a barbarous war with which the frontier was being threatened. He was kept in confinement until in November, 1779, when he was sent to Germantown on parole, and on July 4, 1780, was allowed to go to New York, under pledge of doing or saying nothing injurious to the United States and of conducting himself as a prisoner of war should do. Nevertheless, he promptly submitted plans to Sir Henry Clinton for employing provincial troops and Indian auxiliaries in attacking the frontier outposts, seizing Pittsburgh, fortifying the Alleghenies, and otherwise promoting the royal cause in that region. By April 3, 1781, the only progress Connolly appears to have made towards realizing these ambitious projects was in enlisting 58 Loyal Foresters; and when Clinton proposed to commission him lieutenant colonel commandant in the Queen's Rangers, he accepted the commission and sailed with that corps for Yorktown, Va. On his arrival at Yorktown, Connolly was appointed by Cornwallis to the command of the Virginia and North Carolina Loyalists, with a detachment of the York Volunteers, and was sent to protect the inhabitants of the peninsula formed by the James River and Chesapeake Bay. Late in September he was again taken prisoner, but after Cornwallis's surrender was permitted by the governor of Virginia to return to Philadelphia, where he arrived, December 12th. At the end of the same month Connolly was brought before the Supreme Executive Council of Pennsylvania, on the charge of having violated his parole in Virginia, and was committed to the common jail, inasmuch as his going at large would be "dangerous to the public welfare

and safety." With him was incarcerated one of his Loyal Foresters, James Lewis, who attended him as a servant. Connolly remained in prison until March 1, 1782, when through the efforts
of friends he was permitted to withdraw to New York, on condition of his going to England. This condition he fulfilled "when the
fleet sailed." In his *Narrative* Colonel Connolly tells us that the
recruits he had raised in Virginia, together with the officers he
had warranted for his intended regiment, shared the fate of Cornwallis's army at Yorktown, and that those recruits (Loyal Foresters) who had remained at New York, "as soon as the war became merely defensive, were drafted into another corps." The
misfortunes of Connolly and his intimates served to block, not once
but several times, a plot that American historians agree was the
most formidable Tory enterprise ever concocted against the back
country during the entire revolutionary period, and one which,
if successful, might have produced grave consequences for the
American cause in general.[2]

There were, however, other Tory enterprises besides Connolly's, which aimed at the reduction of the country on the upper
Ohio. One of these was revealed late in August, 1777, to Colonel
Thomas Gaddis of Westmoreland County, Pa., who in turn
warned Lieutenant Colonel Thomas Brown at Redstone Old Fort
on the Monongahela that the local Tories had associated for the
purpose of cutting off the other inhabitants. While Brown kept
guard over his powder magazine and sent word to the patriots to
be "upon their watch," Gaddis and Colonel Zackwell Morgan of
Monongalia County, Va., at once led out the militia, together with
some unenlisted men, in search of the Loyalists; and by August
29, Colonel Morgan was able to report that he had already captured numbers of associators, who confessed that they were in
league with certain leading men at Fort Pitt and were awaiting
a concerted attack by a force of British, French, and Indians on
that post, which was then to be surrendered with but little opposition. Some of those involved in this plot fled to the mountains.
Among these was Henry Maggee of the Perth Valley in Cumberland County, who resorted with thirty others to the fastnesses of
the Alleghenies. Some years later Maggee made an affidavit that,

---

[2] Siebert, "The Tories of the Upper Ohio" in *Bien. Report, Arch. and Hist., W. Va.,
1911-1914*, 41; *Pa. Mag. of Hist. and Biog.*, Apr., 1889, 154-166; Oct., 1889, 281-286; *Colon.
Records of Pa.*, X, 461, 470; XI, 196; XIII, 160, 163. *Papers read before the Lancaster Co.
Hist. Soc.*, VII, No. 6, 126; *Sec. Rep., Bur. of Archives, Ont.*, Pt. II. 1144-1146; Rev. W. O.
Raymond's Ms. Notes from the Muster Rolls of the Provincial Corps; *Am. Arch.*, 4th Ser.,
IV, 88, 104, 112, 155, 479, 508, 598, 617; V, 1119, 1121, 1122; VI, 433, 434, 435.

in conjunction with his friends, he had induced 431 men to sign for enlistment in Butler's Rangers, whose headquarters were at Fort Niagara, but that these recruits were obliged to disperse when one of their number turned informer. Maggee first went to Philadelphia and in 1778 to Nova Scotia. It is not unlikely that William Pickard and his two sons of Westmoreland County signed Maggee's agreement, for we find them joining Butler's Rangers in 1777. Alexander Robertson, an Indian trader, who was one of those caught planning to destroy the powder magazine on the upper Ohio, also fled in the same year.[3]

The closing scene in the conspiracy of 1777 was enacted at Pittsburgh, March 28, 1778, when Captain Alexander McKee, Matthew Elliott, Simon Girty, Robert Surphlitt, John Higgins, and McKee's two negroes made their escape. Captain McKee was the deputy superintendent of Indian Affairs at Fort Pitt, Surphlitt was his cousin, and Higgins appears to have been one of his servants. Simon Girty had long acted as interpreter for the Six Nations. During a considerable time both McKee and Girty had been regarded as suspicious characters and, after an investigation into the alarming situation on the Western frontier by a commission appointed by Congress, these two men and one other had been placed under arrest for a brief period in the autumn of 1777. In Matthew Elliott, who was an Indian trader, the little party of fugitives had a guide who knew the route to Detroit. The trail followed by these Loyalists led through what is now southern Ohio, by way of Coshocton and Old Chillicothe on the west bank of the Scioto River (the site of the present village of Westfall) and thence through the Wyandot towns on the Sandusky River to their destination. At the Shawnee village of Old Chillicothe McKee and his followers found James Girty, whom they persuaded to join them later at Detroit. Shortly after their arrival at this British post, Lieutenant Governor Henry Hamilton appointed McKee deputy agent for Indian Affairs, Elliott captain in the Indian Department, and Simon Girty interpreter and agent in the secret service. Thus, these men were afforded full opportunity to instigate and take a leading part in operations against the frontier

---

[3]Thwaites and Kellogg, *Frontier Defense on the Upper Ohio*, X, 14, 21-24, 33-42, 46, 51-53, 54-68, 70, 142-145, 184-187, 250; *Jour. of Cong.* (new ed.), IX, 831, 942-944, 1018; *Sec. Rep. Bur. of Archives, Ont.*, (1904), Pt. I, 587; Pt. II, 963, 964; Pt. I, 150.

which they had left but recently.' That there were other accessions at Detroit of Loyalists from Pittsburgh during this period
appears probable from the statement of Brigadier General Edward
Hand, who wrote from the latter post, April 24, 1778, to General
Horatio Gates, complaining that since the 18th of the preceding
January forty men had deserted from his small garrison, including
fourteen who had disappeared on the night of April 23d, taking
with them a party of the country people. Hand added that he had
detached four officers and forty men in pursuit. One of the forty
deserters to whom Hand referred was Henry Butler, who arrived
at Kaskasia on the Mississippi near the close of the preceding
February. James Girty made his appearance at Detroit in August,
1778, and was at once appointed interpreter for the Shawnee.
Nearly a year later George Girty came in. He had been a prisoner
for twelve months at New Orleans, whence he had journeyed by
a long and arduous path through the Indian country. He also was
made an interpreter in the Indian Department at Detroit.[5]

The numerous flights from Pittsburgh and its vicinity since
the days of Dunmore's War had removed those Loyalists best qualified to lead in regaining control of the upper Ohio for the Crown.
Connolly, McKee, and the others had thenceforth to labor under
the great disadvantage of forming their plots and attempting their
expeditions at long range against a foe that was familiar with
their purposes and methods, and that was ever alert to thwart
them. There was still, however, a considerable body of Tories on
the upper Ohio, despite the desertions of March and April, 1778,
from Fort Pitt. With the spread of the rumor in the early part
of 1779 that the Loyalists and Indians at Detroit were preparing
to penetrate to Pittsburgh, Hugh Kelly of Maryland betook himself to the neighboring Red Stone settlement and enlisted 175 men;
while his associate, James Fleming of Frederick County, Va.,
raised 75 recruits at Kittanning. According to the formal statement that was submitted by Fleming and Kelly to the authorities
in London toward the end of the Revolution, the work of organiz-
ing the Loyalists was extended by them into the adjacent portions
of Maryland and Virginia, through the agency of Adam Graves,

⁴ Thwaites and Kellogg, *Frontier Defense on the Upper Ohio*, 249-255, 260, n. 14; *Hecke-
welder's Narrative*, 182; Thwaites and Kellogg, *Rev. on the Upper Ohio*, 74, 75; *Sec. Rep.,
Bur. of Archives, Ont.*, (1904), Pt. II, 985, 987, 988, 1082, 1282.

⁵ Thwaites and Kellogg, *Frontier Defense on the Upper Ohio*, 247, 278, 279, 286, 234,
n., 98; *Sec. Rep., Bur. of Archives*, (1904), Pt. II, 988, 1284.

John George Graves, and Nicholas Andrews, all of Maryland, with the result that up to June, 1781, nearly 1,300 volunteers were bound by oath to serve at call in a corps which they proposed to name the Maryland Royal Retaliators. Curiously enough, our informants nowhere intimate that they had received commissions authorizing them to embody these men; and since the enlistment of the proposed corps never got beyond the provisional stage—according to their own admission—we can find no record of it in the Muster Rolls of the Loyalist, or Provincial, Regiments. According to the plan of campaign, as developed by the summer of 1781, General Johnson was to operate with a large force in the neighborhood of Pittsburgh, and Colonel Connolly was to return from the region north of the James River and assist Johnson. Large numbers of British prisoners confined in Winchester, Strasburg, Leesburg, Sharpsburg, Fort Frederick, and Fredericktown, Va., were to be released; the Tories of Somerset and Worcester counties on the Eastern Shore of Maryland were to be aided, should their petition meet with favor, by an expedition to be sent by General Leslie from Portsmouth, Va., to the Chesapeake, and the sea coast was to be molested by the privateers of the Associated Loyalists sent out from New York.

This extended plan, as it happened, broke down at two points: the appeal of the Eastern Shore Tories to General Leslie was intercepted; and the papers revealing the project and names of the Loyalist leaders of Frederick County were delivered by mistake to an American officer in Fredericktown, with the result—according to Kelly and Fleming's account—that 170 of their associates were at once arrested. Of these, Adam and John George Graves, Nicholas Andrews, and four others were tried before a special court, July 25, 1781, and found guilty of high treason. Three of the seven were executed at Fredericktown; Andrews, the two Graves brothers, and Fleming managed in some manner to escape to Cornwallis at Yorktown, whence they were fortunate enough to find their way to New York after the surrender, which occurred on October 19, 1781. At New York they found Kelly, who had preceded them thither. Meanwhile, the General Court at Annapolis rendered the judgment of outlawry against about 100 leading Loyalists, some of whom were from Baltimore County, and at later periods against about 80 others from various localities in

Maryland, including Frederick, Charles, Kent, Montgomery, Somerset, and Worcester counties.[6]

With the exception of several of the leaders, it is impossible to trace the fugitives from the upper Ohio to the localities where they settled after the return of peace. Hugh Kelly was in Halifax in December, 1785, where he made representations of his losses before one of the British Commissioners on Loyalist Claims; and it is probable that one or more of his intimates and some of his followers were also in Nova Scotia. Alexander McKee, Simon Girty, and a few of the Loyalists who had taken refuge at Fort Detroit secured deeds from the Ottawa Indians to Colchester and Gosfield townships on the shore of Lake Erie east of the Detroit River, and opened them to settlement. The transfer of "The Two Connected Townships" thus effected was irregular, and had to be rectified by a reconveyance of the districts from the Indians to the Canadian Government. In 1788 the two townships were laid out in one hundred and nine lots, and during the next five years the settlers who had previously entered the tract were confirmed in the possession of their properties. Thus, arose "The New Settlement," which began about five miles east of the Detroit River and extended for a distance three times as great along the lake front to the eastward. Some of those who drew lots in the two townships did not locate there, going instead to the River Thames, where the soil was of a better quality; while others, to the number of a hundred or more, became discouraged on account of the long delays in obtaining provisions and tools from the government, and returned to the United States. The region next to the Detroit River remained for a time unsettled, partly because of its marshy character and partly on account of doubtful claims. In January, 1793, however, John Graves Simcoe, formerly colonel of the Queen's Rangers, one of the Loyalist Corps, and now lieutenant governor of Ontario, took action, along with his council, by which this tract was constituted the township of Malden and was granted to Alexander McKee, Matthew Elliott, and Captain William Caldwell. The settlers who had already made improvements in the new township were secured in their holdings at the same time.

---

[6] *Rep. on Am. Mss. in Roy. Inst. of Gt. Brit.*, III, 6. 46, 47; I, 20; IV, 241; *Sec. Rep., Bur. of Archives, Ont.*, (1904), Pt. I, 55, 56; Scharf, *Hist. of Md.*, II, 366-368; Siebert, "The Tories of the Upper Ohio" in *Bien. Rep., Archives and Hist., W. Va.*, (1911-1914), 45, 46.

Captain Caldwell, it may be added, was one of Colonel John Butler's Rangers from Fort Niagara.[7]

---

[7] *Sec. Rep., Bur. of Archives, Ont.* (1904), Pt. I, 55; *Third Rep., Bur. of Archives, Ont.* (1905), 222, 223; Siebert, "The Dispersion of the American Tories," in the *Miss. Valley Hist. Rev.,* I, 189, 190.

CHAPTER II

THE LOYALISTS OF NORTHEASTERN PENNSYLVANIA

There was a considerable Loyalist element among the early settlers on the upper Delaware and upper Susquehanna rivers in northeastern Pennsylvania. This was especially true of the Germans of the Susquehanna, among whom the proportion of Loyalists was larger, so far as our scanty evidence indicates, than among their neighbors of the English and Irish nationalities. Various things suggest that the strife between the Whigs and Tories of Tryon County, New York, which centered at Johnstown in the lower Mohawk Valley and resulted in the flight of the Johnsons to Canada in August, 1775, was not without effect beyond the southern boundary of the Province. One of the refugees from Johnstown was John Butler, who was sent by the Canadian authorities to Fort Niagara in the following November. Other Loyalists also made their way to this British outpost, including John Depue, who arrived during the winter of 1776-77, bringing letters from seventy of his neighbors on the Susquehanna proposing to enlist as rangers under Butler's command. This seems to have been the first suggestion of the formation of a corps of armed frontiersmen and raiders at Niagara; although it was not the first time that Butler had held communication with these persons, for he had already invited them to come to the fort. Among the earliest of the group to enter the ranks of the new regiment were Depue himslf, Frederick Auger and his two sons, and Hendrick Windron. Mr. Windron relates that he was accompanied on his journey from the Susquehanna to Niagara by his wife and children and several other families of Loyalists.[1]

In the spring of 1777, not long after the Pennsylvania Assembly had passed an act defining treason and misprision of treason, Philip Bender and the Loyalists of his settlement made the long and arduous journey of several hundred miles to Fort Niagara. Others who testify that they went in the same year are

---

[1] Siebert, "The Loyalists and Six Nation Indians in the Niagara Peninsula" in *Trans. Roy. Soc. Can.*, IX (1915), 80, 81, and references there given.

William Pickard and his two sons, Casper Hover and his three sons, Abraham Wartman, Conrad Sills, Henry Lyman, William Vanderlip, and George Kentner, all of whom enlisted in the Rangers. It is very probable that some of these were members of the party with which Philip Bender went, and that the fathers of families were accompanied not merely by their older sons but also by their wives and younger children. We learn of but one recruit from the Susquehanna in St. Leger's expedition, namely, Philip Buck, who joined it at Fort Stanwix, although there may have been others. In 1778 the movement to Niagara continued with the flight of John Wintermute, Thomas Millard and his three sons, Edward Turner and his father, evidently with other families, and Michael Thomas.

This exodus from the Susquehanna country had not been left to run its own course, but had been stimulated by the recruiting operations of Depue and the Mohawk chieftain, Joseph Brant, after the defeat of St. Leger. These activities are explained by the fact that Butler did not receive permission to organize his corps until after the catastrophe at Fort Stanwix. They were not confined, however, to the upper Susquehanna, nor to the autumn of 1777; for early in the following year Brant invaded the valley of the upper Delaware and gathered in sixty or seventy of the inhabitants of that region, while at the time of his descent on Wyoming in the following summer, Butler gained an accession of forty more Delaware Valley Loyalists. From the fort at Wyoming he released a party of adherents of the Crown, which took the Indian trail through the forest to Oswego, and, embarking thence in row boats, reached Niagara after spending nine days on the waters of Lake Ontario. Doubtless, the other refugees pursued much the same route, or accompanied their rescuers on the march back to Fort Niagara. By 1779 the Tory population of the upper Susquehanna appears to have largely vanished, for we have the record of only one flight from this region in the year just named, that of Isaac Dobson. As Dobson had been imprisoned, he was prevented from leaving earlier.[2]

Numbers of these Loyalists from northeastern Pennsylvania enlisted in the Rangers, as we have observed above; and not a few of them served under Colonel Butler throughout the Revolutionary

---

[2] Siebert, "The Loyalists and Six Nation Indians in the Niagara Peninsula" in *Trans. Roy. Soc. Can.*, IX (1915), 82-86, and references there given.

War. Probably most of them received grants of land in the Niagara Peninsula at the close of the contest, as did the men of Butler's corps in general and the warriors of the Six Nations, who had made Fort Niagara their base of operations since the fall of 1777. A few of the Pennsylvanians, however, soon drifted to other localities; and individuals among them were to be found living a few years after the war at Fort Erie, at Detroit, on the Bay of Quinté, in the Fourth and Fifth townships on the north side of the St. Lawrence River, and at Montreal. In 1787 John Depue was a resident at Fort Erie.[3]

---

[3] *See. Rep., Bur. of Archives, Ont.*, (1904), Pt. I, 831, 480; Pt. II, 963, 968, 970, 973, 974, 975, 981, 984, 990, 997, 1001, 1008, 1262, 1263; *Trans. Roy. Soc. Can.*, IX (1915), 95, ff., 117, ff.

CHAPTER III

THE REPRESSION OF THE LOYALISTS AND NEUTRALS IN SOUTHEASTERN PENNSYLVANIA

In the early months of 1775 the division of sentiment in Pennsylvania over the question of resistance to the Crown was already manifest. The Convention of provincial delegates, which was then in session, approved of open resistance; and Philadelphians suspected of loyal proclivities were being silenced or driven out almost daily by means of advertisements, handbills, or personal warnings which, if unheeded, were followed in extreme cases by the application of tar and feathers. At the same time, the Meeting for Sufferings of Pennsylvania and New Jersey Quakers issued a testimony against usurpation of authority and against insurrections, conspiracies, and illegal assemblies, this last expression being obviously intended to include the provincial conventions and the Continental Congress itself. It would be a mistake, however, to suppose that the Meeting for Sufferings voiced the convictions of all members of the dominant sect in Pennsylvania; for many of them quietly gave financial support to the Revolution, and some deviated from the principle of non-resistance to the extent of joining the association for defending with arms the lives, liberty, and property of the people, entering military organizations, and signing the test that was later prescribed by Congress and the State.[1]

The news from Lexington, which was received in Philadelphia five days after the battle, seems to have produced a marked effect upon the "Tory class" there, according to the *Diary* or *Remembrancer* of Christopher Marshall, a Quaker patriot of the city, who noted on May 7 that "Their language is quite softened, and many of them have so far renounced their former sentiments as that they have taken up arms, and are joined in the association; nay even many of the stiff Quakers, and some of those who drew up the Testimony are ashamed of their proceedings." It was, indeed, soon after this that a number of young Friends formed a company of light infantry in the American interest, which was

---

[1] Scharf and Westcott, *Hist of Phila.*, I, 293, 294, 296, n. 1.

under the command of Sheriff Joseph Cowperthwait, and was called the "Quaker Blues." Not inconsistent with Marshall's statement regarding the changed conduct of the Philadelphia Loyalists were the observations of Judge Samuel Curwen, a fugitive Tory from Salem, Mass., who spent the week of May 5-12 in the Quaker City. In his search for lodgings, Curwen became convinced that the place was pervaded with "congressional principles" to such a degree that no man there dared express a doubt concerning the feasibility of the projects of Congress, and that the inhabitants were displeased with New Englanders for making the town their haven of refuge. These views and the advice of his friend Judge Joseph Lee, a lukewarm Tory of Cambridge, Mass., who was leading the life of a recluse in Philadelphia, induced Mr. Curwen to re-embark, this time for London, Eng., where he arrived on July 3.[2]

Meantime, in keeping with the suggestion of Benjamin Franklin, a Committee of Safety supplanted the Committee of Correspondence on June 30, being given discretionary powers by the Pennsylvania Assembly. In employing these powers it dealt more severely with suspected and inimical persons than its predecessor had done. The new committee required well-known or self-acknowledged Loyalists, like Amos Wickersham, Mordecai Levy, John Bergen, and Thomas Loosley, to confess and recant their errors; and it was soon ordered by Congress to prevent the departure of all persons who were likely to do injury to the American cause. On August 12, the committee compelled Terence McDermot, "a volunteer" in the King's army, and two officers, who were on their way to join the British forces in Boston, to sign an agreement not to bear arms against the United Colonies for one year or until exchanged; after which they were conveyed to Washington's camp at Cambridge, Mass. Isaac Hunt, who was defending a suit for the replevin of some forbidden goods for the avowed Loyalist, William Conn, was summoned before the Committee of Inspection; but on refusing to discontinue the suit or apologize, he was carted through the streets behind a drum and fife playing the Rogue's March. The procession stopped before the home of Dr. John Kearsley, Jr., an uncompromising Tory, who became so furious at the spectacle that he snapped his pistol at the crowd. Mr. Hunt

---

[2] Scharf and Westcott, *Hist. of Phila.*, I, 300, 301; Duane, ed., *Extracts from the Diary of Christopher Marshall;* Sargent, ed., *Loyal Verses of Jos. Stansbury and Dr. Jonathan Odell*, 133; Curwin, *Journal and Letters*, 25-30, 487.

appears to have seized this opportunity to ask the pardon of his persecutors, who released him and mounted Kearsley upon the cart in his place. Hunt soon after fled to England; and although his substitute was let go without an apology, which he refused to give, he was apprehended, together with several others, early in October, on the evidence of certain intercepted letters, which showed that he was endeavoring to bring about an invasion of Pennsylvania by the British troops, besides engaging in other inimical practices. After trial by the Committee of Safety Kearsley was sent to York as a prisoner and died there during the war. The largest group of Loyalists that the committee ordered imprisoned during this year was brought in at the end of October from the New Jersey shore. It comprised Captain Duncan Campbell, Lieutenant James S. Symes, and twenty-three privates of the Royal Highland Emigrants, a corps but recently formed, who were stranded while on their voyage from Boston to New York, were captured, and brought before the committee in Philadelphia. They were incarcerated in the jail and workhouse, the first prisoners of war to be confined in the Quaker City during the Revolution.[2]

Regardless of the suspicions already existing, and certain to be increased, concerning their neutrality, the Quakers, Menonists, and Dunkards or German Baptists, who enjoyed certain exemptions at the hands of Congress, memorialized the Pennsylvania Assembly at this time in opposition to the general order for the enrollment of the militia. Thereupon, the Committee of Safety marched to the State House, carrying a remonstrance against the Quaker address, which was declared to present an aspect unfriendly to the liberties of America and destructive of society and government. The remonstrance further alleged that "these gentlemen want to withdraw their persons and their fortunes from the service of the country at a time when their country stands most in need of them." The association also sent in a remonstrance, denouncing leniency to the lukewarm as nothing less than a fatal mistake. At length, in November, the Assembly went on record by making defensive service compulsory and "taxing all non-associators £2 10s above the regular assessment." This action, along with other developments of the time, only served to embolden the

² Colon. Records of Pa., X, 280, 302, 342, 343, 359, 360, 367, 372, 373, 380, 385, 386, 410; Raymond, ed., Winslow Papers, 42, n.; Rep. on Am. Mss. in the Roy. Inst. of G. Brit., II, 79; Scharf and Westcott, Hist. of Phila., I, 295, 303.

Quakers, for their Yearly Meeting published a testimony, which was adopted January 20, 1776, advising the members of the society to stand firm in their allegiance and unite against every design of independence. Not content with testimonies and memorials, Quaker merchants and traders, as well as a few others, were in some instances required to apologize for breaches of the regulations established by the Committee of Inspection relating to the admission and prices of commodities, especially of foodstuffs; while in other instances they were denounced as enemies and excluded from all trade or intercourse with the other inhabitants, because they refused to accept Continental currency.[4]

Besides these local offenders who were dealt with by the two committees, there were others from distant parts of the Province or from other Colonies who had been captured and sent to Congress for adequate punishment, and were handed over by that body to the Committee of Safety for examination and sentence or for incarceration, as the case might be. Of such were some of the Tory prisoners who were transferred from the old prison to the new one in Philadelphia in January, 1776, including the notorious Dr. John Connolly and his two confederates, Dr. John Ferdinand Dalziel Smyth of Maryland and Allen Cameron of the Cherokee country, besides Colonel Moses Kirkland of South Carolina, who had been taken on his voyage to Boston; General Donald McDonald, chief of the North Carolina Tories; Colonel Allen McDonald, and "twenty-five more of their set." In the following May, Colonel Kirkland was enabled to escape by the aid of several local Loyalists, including Arthur Thomas and his sons, who were constrained to flee when a mob attacked their house. Mr. Thomas tells us that he avoided seizure by taking his departure in the night, that he remained in concealment for several weeks, but was caught in July and imprisoned. He also says that he succeeded in getting away to New York in the following September. A year later, however, Mr. Thomas returned to Philadelphia, on learning that the British army had taken possession of the city. Arthur Thomas, Jr., was also caught and imprisoned. Besides the Thomases, other Tories, either singly or in small groups, were brought before the Committee of Safety during the year 1776, thirty-three of these being secured in New York in October.[5]

[4] Scharf and Westcott, *Hist of Phila.*, I, 302, 305.

[5] *Ibid.*, 305, 326; *2d Rep., Bur. of Archives, Ont.* (1904), Pt. I, 613; *Colon. Records of Pa.*, X, 461, 466, 469, 470, 472, 477, 485, 502, 616, 618, 638, 661, 662, 676, 731, 756, 773.

Meanwhile, the outspoken Loylists of other communities in the State were being looked after by their local committees of safety. Thus, for example, on July 21, 1775, John Huff, Thomas Meredith, and Thomas Smith were reported to the committee of Bucks County as having uttered expressions derogatory to the American cause. Huff at once appeared before the committee, acknowledged the charge, and made such concessions as were deemed a sufficient atonement. The accusations against the other two men were referred to a sub-committee for investigation, and on August 21, Meredith's written apology was read, accepted, and ordered published. In it the writer not only repented of what he had done, but also "voluntarily" renounced his former principles and promised henceforth to render his conduct unexceptionable to his countrymen by strictly adhering to the measures of Congress. Thomas Smith of Upper Makefield was much less submissive than his offending brethren. At first he denied most of what was alleged against him; but the committee, refusing to be satisfied with this, proceeded to examine several witnesses, as well as the defendant himself, and then ordered the statement published that Mr. Smith had declared in substance, "That the Measures of Congress had already enslaved America and done more Damage than all the Acts of Parliament ever intended to lay upon us, that the whole was nothing but a scheme of a parcel of hot-headed Presbyterians and that he believed the Devil was at the bottom of the whole; that the taking up Arms was the most scandalous thing a man could be guilty of and more heinous than an hundred of the grossest offences against the moral law, etc., etc., etc." Together with these opinions of the accused, the committee's sentence was also to be published, namely, that "the said Thomas Smith be considered as an Enemy of the Rights of British America, and that all persons break off every kind of dealing with him until he shall make proper satisfaction to this Committee for his conduct." Before this case appeared in the press, Thomas Smith expressed his penitence and remorse and presented a satisfactory recantation in writing to the committee. Other instances, in which, however, submission was always promptly made, are scattered through the minutes of the committee until July, 1776. From the first of that month until the 12th of August, when the records come to an abrupt conclusion, the last four meetings of the committee dealt with a few offences committed by Loyalists against the resolutions passed by the Assembly early in the preceding April, which provided for the disarming of disaffected persons and non-associators and the supplying of the confiscated arms to such Continental troops as should be raised in the Colony.[6]

Towards the end of April, 1776, the election for members of the General Assembly was held. The result of the canvass in Philadelphia, which had been preceded by much excitement, was of especial significance. By a combination of the local Tories and Moderates, or as Christopher Marshall summed up the elements of the coalition, "the Quakers, papists, church, Allen family, with all the proprietary party," the Whigs were beaten. In reality, however, as was soon to appear, the Tories and their friends had overreached themselves. The patriots were now more than ever determined to overthrow the charter and the proprietary government, and to establish in its place a government founded on majority rule. Independence was already recognized by the opposing parties to be the definite object of the war.[7]

With the development of these conditions in Philadelphia, some of the influential conservatives turned from public affairs in the city in order to seek retirement in outlying villages. Others of no political prominence, but whose minds were equally filled with fears, removed with their families to places that promised greater personal security than did the capital. Thus, early in May, 1776, Thomas Bartow, a merchant of Philadelphia, took his wife and five children to Bethlehem, where he made his home for the next three years. Of the four sons of Chief Justice William Allen—brothers-in-law of Governor John Penn—James withdrew with his small family to Allentown in Northampton County, June 16; John and his family went about the same time to Union Iron Works in Hunterdon County, N. J.; Andrew retired soon after to his place at Neshaminy, and William, returning from Ticonderoga shortly after the Declaration of Independence, resigned his commission as lieutenant-colonel of militia.[8]

But most of the Tory residents continued in Philadelphia and, as they had held their political meetings before the election, so now they held congratulatory and convivial sessions. At the end of May, the Committee of Safety received confidential information

[6] Pa. Mag. of Hist. and Biog., XV, 263, 265-270, 273, 275, 277, 279-281, 283, 285, 286, 289, 290.

[7] Scharf and Westcott, Hist. of Phila., I, 311.

[8] Pa. Mag. of Hist. and Biog., Jan., 1889, 388; July, 1885, 187, 190 191; Am. Arch., 5th Ser., III, 1280, 1281, 1377, 1397, 1434.

according to Marshall's *Diary*, of not less than four different Tory clubs that were meeting frequently, one at the Widow Ball's in Lombard Street, another at the sign of the Pennsylvania Farmer, the third at Jones's beer house on the dock, and the fourth at the sign of the King's Arms. The impartation of this piece of information led to the immediate appointment of a Committee of Secrecy, including Mr. Marshall and seven others, to examine all inimical and suspected persons of whom the committee might learn. The labors of the new committee resulted in a number of arrests and imprisonments, among those committeed being James Prescott, William Smith, Joseph Stansbury (the Tory poet), David Shoemaker, and others.[9]

Early in June, 1776, the Committee of Inspection was engaged in correspondence with the local committees of safety for the purpose of having them send some of their members to the Provincial Conference, which was to meet in Philadelphia on the 18th to arrange for the election of members to a Constitutional Convention. On July 8 this election was held, and later in the same month the Convention met to frame a constitution for Pennsylvania. Under the guiding hand of its president, Benjamin Franklin, the Convention supplanted the General Assembly, which finally passed out of existence on September 26. On July 19 it passed an ordinance requiring the commanding officers of the militia to appraise and take over such arms as the non-associators in their respective districts had failed to deliver up according to the earlier resolutions of Congress and the Provincial Assembly, and to arm the associators with the weapons thus secured. During the early days of September the Convention passed two ordinances that were intended to limit the dangerous activities of the Loyalists. The first of these declared that every person owing allegiance to the State who, after the publication of the present decree, should levy war against the Commonwealth or give aid to the enemy, either within the State or elsewhere, and be convicted thereof, should be adjudged guilty of high treason and should forfeit his lands, tenements, goods, and chattels, besides being imprisoned for any term not exceeding the duration of the war. The second ordinance provided that any person within the State, who should endeavor by writing or speaking to obstruct the measures of the United States

---

⁹ Sargent, ed., *Loyal Verses of Jos. Stansbury and Dr. Jonathan Odell*, 117, 122; Duane, ed., *Extracts from the Diary of Christopher Marshall*, 80, 81.

in defense of freedom, should, on the production of proper proof, give security for his good behavior, or stand committed until the security was forthcoming, or he was otherwise legally discharged. If, however, the offender was considered to be too dangerous for release by bail, the justice was to associate with himself two other justices of the neighborhood, and they together were to fix the term of imprisonment, provided it did not extend beyond the end of the war. The Convention also deposed Governor John Penn, and ignored the proprietary government. Meanwhile, it had elected a Council of Safety on July 22, thus dissolving the Committee of Safety; but it did not disturb the Committee of Inspection for the present. The Council of Safety continued to exercise its functions until March 4, 1777, when the Supreme Executive Council, which was provided for in the constitution, assumed control.[10]

There was, then, to be no respite for the Tories and suspected persons in Pennsylvania; and in truth the Tories did not conduct themselves in such a way, after the adoption of the Declaration of Independence by Congress, as to conciliate the revolutionary party. They exposed themselves to the danger of arrest, and were incarcerated daily. Furthermore, their position was made the more difficult by the action of the new Assembly, which proceeded on February 11, 1777, to supply somewhat fuller definitions of treason and misprision of treason than the Constitutional Convention had done in the preceding September. In the middle of July numbers of Whig associators were sent into New Jersey to help defend that region against the anticipated British invasion. It was not, however, until the beginning of November that Howe began his march into the Jerseys, signalizing the event by a proclamation of amnesty to individuals, which he repeated at Trenton on November 30. These proclamations, with the gloomy outlook for the American cause, are said to have induced some 3,000 Jersey farmers to swear allegiance to the Crown; but their effect reached beyond the domain of the invaded Province. Thus, for example, in October, Gilbert Hicks of Bucks County fled to Shrewsbury, N. J., and in the following month to Trenton; but after Rahl's defeat at the latter place, January 2, 1777, he took refuge among some Tory families, until it was safe for him to enter Philadelphia. Shortly after Rahl's defeat, the Council of Safety adopted a resolution de-

---

[10] *Pa. Mag. of Hist. and Biog.*, XV, 279; *Statutes at Large of Pa.*, IX, 11-12, 18-19; *Laws of Pa.*, II, 144-147; Scharf and Westcott, *Hist. of Phila.*, I, 316, 322, 323.

claring that every person who was so devoid of honor, virtue, and love of his country as to refuse his assistance "at this time of eminent public danger" might be suspected of designs inimical to the freedom of America, and that where such designs were very apparent from the conduct of individuals, they ought to be confined during the absence of the militia. The officers of the State were directed to act accordingly, reserving appeals to the Council. It was the enforcement of this resolution that caused what James Allen called in his *Diary* a persecution of the Tories, when—to use his own words—"houses were broken open, people imprisoned without any color of authority by private persons, and as was said a list of 200 disaffected persons [was] made out, who were to be seized, and imprisoned and sent off to North Carolina." In this list the Allens were reported to be included. Under such an apprehension, Andrew and William joined their brother John at Union Iron Works, and the three brothers were not long in deciding to claim the protection of Howe's army at Trenton. Thence, they proceeded to New York City, leaving their families behind them. Many more influential citizens are said to have gone over to the enemy at this time. One of these was Joseph Galloway, the talented, wealthy, and prominent lawyer of Philadelphia who, after being visited by mobs that threatened him with a coat of tar and feathers and even with hanging, loaded some valuables into a wagon, quitted his country home at Trevose, and in company with several other notable Loyalists, made his way to the British camp at New Brunswick, N. J. James Allen, who had been bringing suspicion on himself by entertaining British officers at Allentown and in other ways, was arrested on December 19 by an armed guard, which took him before the Council of Safety at Philadelphia, where he pledged his honor "not to say or do anything injurious to the Cause of America." After remaining in and about the city for several days and noting that the place "seemed almost deserted and resembled a Sunday in service time," he returned to Allentown. The cause of this deserted appearance in the town was, of course, the fear that Howe would cross the Delaware and take possession of Philadelphia. About the only people who had not surrendered to the intense excitement of the hour and driven away with their household goods in such vehicles as could be had to places of refuge were some of the Tories and the Quakers. In the latter part of December, the Society of Friends had indeed issued their usual testimony urging the faithful to exercise a patient spirit and Christian fortitude in refusing to submit "to the arbitrary injunctions and ordinances of men who assume to themselves the power of compelling others, either in person or by assistance, to aid in carrying on war."[11]

The imprisonment of Joseph Stansbury and others of his fellow-townsmen at the instigation of the Committee of Secrecy had occurred under such circumstances that the Council of Safety appointed a committee of its own members to inquire into the causes of their commitment, with a view to determining the justice of discharging them in case they would declare their allegiance to the State in writing. This action does not seem to have resulted in the immediate release of those concerned.

Meantime, there had been much desertion among the militia, and when many of the principal men in Colonel Hunter's battalion of Berks County refused going to join Washington's army in January, 1777, the Council ordered the colonel to send the ringleaders among the disaffected to Philadelphia for discipline. That there was also widespread disaffection among the Philadelphians themselves appears from various sources, personal and official. James Allen says that Congress itself complained of this disloyalty, although, as he remarks, the people of the city had been favored with most of its official appointments and with its presence from the beginning. A notable instance of the thing complained of came to light in the early spring of 1777 through the detection of James Molesworth's attempt to bribe pilots to navigate Lord Howe's vessels from New York to Philadelphia. Molesworth, who had been for several years clerk to the mayor of the city, turned out to be a British spy and was hanged on the common on March 31. Five others, who were implicated in this business, made their escape. Others suspected persons and Tories were severely dealt with, among these being Major Richard V. Stockton of the New Jersey Volunteers, "the famous land pilot" to the King's troops, who had been surprised and taken prisoner on February 18, with about three score privates, all of whom were sent to Philadelphia for confinement. Several Delaware Tories, however, were released on giving security.[12]

[11] *Statutes at Large of Pa.*, IX, 45-47; Scharf and Westcott, *Hist. of Phila.*, I, 826, 829, 835; *Colon. Records of Pa.*, XI, 38, 43, 94; *Pa. Mag. of Hist. and Biog.*, July, 1885, 193-195; Oct., 1885, 280, 282, 286, 287; Dec., 1902, 432, 433; *2d Rep., Bur. of Archives, Ont.* (1904), Pt. I, 94; *Am. Arch.* 5th Ser., III, 1434.

[12] Scharf and Westcott, *Hist. of Phila.*, I, 339; Sabine, *Loyalists of the Am. Rev.*, II, 335.

The difficulty of finding quarters for the new levies continually pouring into Philadelphia after the battles of Trenton and Princeton led to an order billeting them on the non-associators, greatly to the dismay of the local Tories. Another measure that proved more generally disturbing to this class of people was the militia bill passed by the Assembly, June 13, 1777, for the purpose of providing troops in place of the associators. It required all white male inhabitants of the State above the age of eighteen years, except those in the extreme western counties, to take the oath of allegiance to Pennsylvania before July 1, 1777, to promise to do nothing to the prejudice of independence, and to expose all conspiracies and treasons that might come within their knowledge. Persons failing to take this oath were declared to be incapable of holding office, serving on juries, suing for debts, transferring real estate, and were liable to be disarmed by the county lieutenants and their deputies, as also to be arrested if traveling outside of their respective cities or counties without a pass.[18] James Allen reports that but few of his neighbors in the County of Northampton subscribed to the oath of allegiance and that they seldom ventured from home because they ran "a risk of being stopt." Some of the leading men of the Moravian congregation at Bethlehem in this county were Tories. Thus, the Reverend George Kribel was compelled to serve a brief term in Easton jail in August, because he refused to abjure the King according to the specific requirements of the militia bill; and John Francis Oberlin was required to resign the custody of the church store after serving as its keeper for many years, because he hotly remarked that he "had sufficient rope in his store to hang all Congress." At the time of the active search for Loyalists in the preceding December, word was brought to Bethlehem that the place had been represented to the American army as a nest of Tories and that General Lee had boasted that "in a few hours he would make an end of Bethlehem." However, the Moravians explained their own position in a petition to Congress declaring that since the outbreak of the conflict they had been continually disturbed for not associating in the use of arms, or acting against their principles in regard to war. They complained that some of them had been imprisoned on account of the test contained in the law of April 1st, that all their able-bodied men above the military age had been heavily fined, and that they found them-

---

[18] *Statutes at Large of Pa.*, IX, 110-114.

selves subject to outlawry and exile without any inquiry into their behavior, although they regarded themselves as accountable to the magistrates. They insisted that they willingly helped to bear the public burdens and that they were ready to furnish reasonable assurance that they would not act against Pennsylvania or any other State, but that they humbly thought themselves entitled to the privileges which had brought them to America, notwithstanding the change in the form of government. These privileges they had not forfeited by any word or act against the new government, they said. At the same time, if the test was to be applied, they must be ruined and their creditors wronged, for it was contrary to their conscience to take the prescribed oath. They would with the help of God act honestly, not fearing the consequences. It may be remarked that as the Moravians had suffered under the militia law of April 1st, they viewed with dismay the enactment of a supplementary measure by the Assembly on June 13, prescribing a new test of allegiance, a measure justified in the eyes of the patriots by the renewed prospect of Howe's advance against Philadelphia. The law of June 13, while it re-enacted most of the provisions of that of the preceding 1st of April, required justices of the peace as the administering officers of the new oath of abjuration of the King and of allegiance to Pennsylvania as an independent State to transmit to the recorders of thier respective counties by October 1 of each year the names of those sworn during the preceding twelve months. Every person above the age of eighteen years who traveled out of the county or city in which he usually resided was to carry a certificate of his allegiance, or be liable to arrest on suspicion and to examination by the nearest justice, who was to tender the oath, which the suspect must take or suffer imprisonment until he would consent to subscribe. The law said that this clause was necessary, in order to prevent the dissemination of discord by persons traveling from one locality to another, and because "this state is already become (and likely to be more so) an asylum for refugees flying from the just resentment of their fellow citizens in other states." It therefore required all newcomers from other Commonwealths to apply at once to the nearest justice for the administering of the oath under the same penalty as was provided in the case of those going from place to place within the State.[14] It was doubtless on

---

[14] *Pa. Mag. of Hist. and Biog.*, Oct., 1885, 287; Scharf and Westcott, *Hist. of Phila.*, I, 341; Jan., 1889, 401, 395, 385, 386; *Laws of Pa.*, II, 154; *Statutes at Large of Pa.*, IX, 110-114.

account of these laws that 160 recruits set out from the city for Staten Island to join the New Jersey Volunteers, a Loyalist corps under the command of Brigadier General Cortlandt Skinner, which had its headquarters there. The party was intercepted, however, near Bawnbrook in the Jerseys, and 60 were taken, including Peter Snider and his brother Elias. The leaders, John Mea and James Stiff, were executed; and the others appear to have been imprisoned for longer or shorter periods, Elias being confined for eighteen months and Peter for six. The two brothers were released on condition that they would serve in the Continental army. Peter did so for three months and then, after hiding out for thirty days, escaped within the lines of Howe's army, now in possession of Philadelphia. Elias secured a furlough on account of sickness, spent a twelvemonth in the woods to avoid recapture, and finally pushed on to Staten Island.[15]

On Sunday, August 24, 1777, Washington at the head of the main body of the Continental army marched through Philadelphia on his way to Wilmington, Del., to meet the British. If, as has been asserted, it was the desire of the commander in chief to impress the Tories, Quakers, and other disaffected persons, he seems to have succeeded at least in part, for according to Allen's *Diary,* many of the townspeople now voluntarily swore allegiance to the new government. Nevertheless, according to Sub-lieutenant John Lacey, who later became a brigadier general in the American service, a formidable number of Tories still existed in the City and County of Philadelphia, as well as in his own County of Bucks. Lacey maintains that a radical change took place in the political sentiments of his neighbors and acquaintances of Bucks after the affair at Trenton, that thereafter they began to manifest "a sullen, vindictive and mal:gnant spirit" which led them to utter threats and menaces when in congenial company, to give secret information to the British, and to attempt dissuading the Whigs from enlisting in the American army and militia. He finds it difficult to decide which party was the more numerous in his county; and although he had been a Quaker himself, he charges that a great part of the disaffected made a plea of conscience in refusing to bear arms, thus affording a local preponderance in favor of the Revolution. Otherwise they did everything they could do, he insists, by encour-

---

[15] *2d Rep., Bur. of Archives, Ont.* (1904), Pt. I, 270.

aging the youth to join the British and by actually sending many of them into the ranks of the enemy.[16]

On August 25th, the day of the landing of the British at the head of Chesapeake Bay on their way to Philadelphia, Congress adopted two resolutions obviously intended as precautionary measures. One of these requested the executive authorities of Pennsylvania and Maryland to cause all notoriously disaffected persons within their respective States to be forthwith apprehended, disarmed, and secured, until they might be released without injury to the common cause. The other recommended to the Supreme Executive Council of Pennsylvania to have the houses of all inhabitants of Philadelphia searched for firearms, swords, and bayonets which, if found, should be paid for at an appraised value and turned over to any of the State militia needing them. Three days after the adoption of these resolutions, Congress, finding symptoms of disaffection among the Quakers of Philadelphia and fearing communication with the enemy and other injurious acts by the disaffected ones, earnestly recommended to the Supreme Executive Council to secure Joshua Fisher and his two sons, Thomas and Samuel, Abel and John James, Israel and James Pemberton, Henry Drinker, Samuel Pleasants, and Thomas Wharton, Sr. The Council at once responded to these measures by directing the commanding officer of each regiment of the city militia to appoint searching parties for the various wards, and by asking the assistance of David Rittenhouse, the treasurer of state, and three military officers in preparing a list of persons dangerous to the Commonwealth, with a view to their arrest and the seizure of any papers of a political nature in their possession, including the records of the Meeting of Sufferings of the Society of Friends, for transmission to Congress. The list, which was drawn up on August 31, contained the names of thirty-one individuals, besides those supplied by Congress. James Allen, who knew many of the designated persons intimately, characterized them as "principal Inhabitants of Philadelphia, chiefly Quakers"; and Robert Proud, the Tory school-master, who also enjoyed the friendship or acquaintance of many of the proscribed, said that they were "mostly Friends," several of whom were "Persons of the first Rank, For-

---

[16] Scharf and Westcott, *Hist. of Phila.*, I, 343; *Pa. Mag. of Hist. and Biog.*, Oct., 1885, 286; Apr., 1902, 101, 104.

tune and Esteem, both in the City and in the Society." As he was writing to his brother, he added that he had had great reason to fear for his own safety, "having not only been obnoxious to the Incendiaries and Usurpers, but also particularly pointed out and threatened by them, more than many others," but that he had escaped molestation by living "in a very private and retired Way, even like a Person dead amidst the Confusions," and communing more with his books than with persons. Among those named in the list were the Reverend William Smith, D.D., provost of the college; the Reverend Thomas Coombs, rector of Christ Church; Samuel Shoemaker; William Drewitt Smith, druggist; Miers Fisher and John Hunt, lawyers; Joseph Fox, late barrack-master; Thomas Ashton, merchant, and Thomas Pike, dancing master.[17]

The committee, which had prepared this list, also named the persons who were to make the arrests. These persons were instructed to apprehend some of the proscribed at once, but to spare the others the mortification of arrest, if they would promise to remain in their homes subject to the order of the Council and would do nothing injurious to the United States. A fourth of the number gave the required promise and were released on parole; one had already taken the oath of allegiance, and another did so; the rest were imprisoned in the Masonic Lodge, as the jails were full, except two or three who could not be found. For some unknown reason, no returns were made in the cases of Joshua Fisher and Provost William Smith. Before any of the prisoners were sent into exile in Virginia, one of their number was released on bail, another was ordered to Connecticut, and a third gave his parole to return to New York. On September 11th, twenty-two finally set out under escort of the City Guard on their way to Winchester, where most of them remained until April 19, 1778, when they were released to return to their homes. However, two had died during the previous month, namely, Thomas Gilpin and John Hunt, and two others had made their escape. One of these was Thomas Pike, the dancing master, who was never heard of again, and the other was William Drewitt Smith, who "rode out to take the air," as his associates supposed, on December 8, 1777, but did not return, preferring to seek protection within the British lines at Philadelphia. Two others, namely, the Reverend Thomas Coombs and Phineas Bond,

---

[17] *Colon. Records of Pa.*, XI, 264, 267, 279, 283, 284, 286-290, 295, 300, 309; Gilpin, *Exiles in Va.*; *Pa. Mag. of Hist. and Biog.*, Jan., 1910, 63.

had been earlier set free in order to embark at a Virginia port for the West Indies, the former being bound for the island of St. Eustatius.[18]

Although the proprietary government had been in abeyance ever since Franklin and the Provincial Convention had assumed control of affairs in the summer of 1776, the officials under the former dispensation had not been taken into custody; but on July 31, 1777, Congress passed a resolution that it was expedient that the late proprietary and Crown office-holders and all other disaffected persons in and near Philadelphia be arrested. This resolution, like the recent recommendations emanating from the same source for the seizure of Loyalists, was comprehensive in its scope. Nevertheless, the Supreme Executive Council set to work issuing warrants for the apprehension of Governor John Penn, Benjamin Chew, who had been a member of Penn's Council and chief justice; James Tilghman, also a member of the Provincial Council; Jared Ingersoll, judge of admiralty; Dr. George Drummond, custom-house officer, and other lesser officials. Penn and Chew were paroled to remain within six miles of their residences; Ingersoll was ordered sent to Winchester, Va., on parole; Tilghman was not to cross the Delaware or depart six miles from it, and the others were confined to their own houses or put in prison. But the Supreme Executive Council was anxious to be relieved of its responsibility for the safe-keeping of Chief Justice Chew and Governor Penn, and therefore requested Congress to remove the distinguished prisoners from the State. That body complied promptly, and a military escort conducted the deposed officials to Fredericksburg, Va. By October 1st, however, according to James Allen, they were transferred to Union Iron Works in New Jersey; and there Mr. Allen visited them early in February, 1778, receiving on the day after his arrival the news of the death at Philadelphia of his brother John, which had occurred on the second of the month.[19]

[18] Gilpin, *Exiles in Va.;* Scharf and Westcott, *Hist. of Phila.,* I, 344, 345, 346.

[19] *Pa. Mag. of Hist. and Biog.,* Oct., 1885, 288, 292; Jan. 1886, 443; Scharf and Westcott, *Hist. of Phila.,* I. 343. 345.

CHAPTER IV

THE BRITISH INVASION OF PENNSYLVANIA
AUGUST 25, 1777, TO JUNE 18, 1778

Andrew and William, brothers of James Allen, were with Howe and his army of 17,000 men when they disembarked, August 25 and 26, 1777, at the head of the Elk River. So also was Joseph Galloway, who had come as adviser to the British commander in chief. The region in which the disembarkation was effected was full of Loyalists, and from the first Howe was supplied with ample intelligence. The presence of these troublesome foes did not escape the attention of Washington, for on August 27th, he mentioned them in a letter addressed from Wilmington to the president of Congress. Among the troops that accompanied Howe were two Tory organizations, the Queen's Rangers and a detachment of the Royal Guides and Pioneers, both of which, especially the former, were to receive many recruits from among the local inhabitants and refugees during the expedition. Indeed, Tories began to come in from the time of the landing, including Dr. John Watson of New Castle, Del., and Hugh McNeal from near Bedford, Pa. The latter has left an affidavit that he made his appearance after being imprisoned for aiding young men in their flight to the army. The British commander encouraged this movement by issuing a proclamation, August 31st, offering protection to such inhabitants as would present themselves and swear allegiance to the Crown within the next sixty days. Refugees continued to come in, although we have no means of knowing in what numbers. From a few individual testimonies we learn that among those who joined the royal force on its march northward were men from Chester County and from Philadelphia. Thus, Captain Alexander McDonald, a Philadelphian, came in with several Loyalists at Wilmington, and entered immediately—according to his own statement—on the task of raising recruits. Curtis Lewis of Chester County joined at Kennett Square, and probably then or soon after Gideon Vernon also of Chester County, and Philip Marchington, a merchant of Philadelphia.[1]

In the middle of September, the Supreme Executive Council received information that the public stores at York, Lancaster, Carlisle, and elsewhere had been destroyed, that men were to be levied in support of the royal cause, and that James Rankin of Manchester, William Willis of Newberry, John Ferree and Daniel Shelly of Lancaster County, and others were concerned in these hostile enterprises. Already Shelly was in custody; and as he offered to tell what he knew against his accomplices he was promised pardon, provided he would divulge enough to convict them. Nine others, who were being held on charges of disaffection, maintained their innocence, and were granted their release on the condition of appearing, if wanted, and abstaining from anything likely to injure the American cause.[2]

Congress and the Assembly stayed in Philadelphia until September 18th, when both bodies adjourned to meet in Lancaster. The Supreme Executive Council did not leave until the 23d of the same month. For several weeks, according to Robert Proud, the revolutionary party had been busy stripping the city of its church bells, supply of lead, and much else that might be useful to the enemy or to the Continental forces. About 4,000 head of cattle were collected from the meadows and from Hog Island by the committee entrusted with that duty and driven away, after which the meadow banks were cut and the pastures inundated. Blankets, clothing, and shoes were exacted from the citizens in spite of Tory protests; magazines and supplies were removed, and the money and papers of the loan office and the records of the State were carried to Easton.[3]

Meantime, the patriots and their families had followed the Council and the legislative bodies into retirement, leaving the Quakers and Loyalists behind. But not all of the patriots or Whigs had departed, as we learn from several sources. On September 25th, one day before Lord Cornwallis entered Philadelphia at the head of 1,500 British and Hessian Grenadiers, Mrs. Henry Drinker

[1] Scharf and Westcott, *Hist. of Phila.*, I, 347; *2d Rep., Bur. of Archives, Ont.* (1904), Pt. I, 253, 295, 494, 611; Pt. II, 900, 1162; *Washington Papers*, I, 178; *Am. Mss. in the Roy. Inst. of Gt. Brit.*, I, 132.

[2] *Colon. Records of Pa.*, XI, 307, 308.

[3] Scharf and Westcott, *Hist. of Phila.*, I, 348, 349, 350; *Pa. Mag. of Hist. and Biog.*, Jan., 1910, 72.

wrote in her *Journal*: "Most of our warm people have gone off"; and Christopher Marshall tells us on what he considered reliable authority that on the same day four or five hundred Tories paraded out to Germantown (where the main army under General Howe first encamped) and, returning, "triumphed through the streets all night," sending to prison such persons as they regarded to be friends of the rebellious States, including "the parson, Jacob Duché." The number imprisoned amounted to "some hundreds," Mrs. Drinker records; although there were other Whigs remaining in the city who were not molested, probably through the friendship of Galloway and the Allens. These refugees from Philadelphia, together with other citizens of the town, arrived with Cornwallis "to the great relief of the inhabitants" who, Robert Morton's *Diary* avers, had "too long suffered the yoke of arbitrary power," and who testified their approbation of the coming of the troops "by loudest acclamations of joy." Whatever the joy of some may have been, there were numerous others whose feelings impelled them to withdraw from the city even after its occupation. On October 1, James Allen observed that some of the inhabitants of Philadelphia were coming up to settle at Allentown and that the road from Easton to Reading was then "the most travelled in America."[4]

That Howe profited by the assistance of local Tories in the course of his advance from the head of the Elk to Germantown can scarcely be doubted. Thus, in the early hours of September 21, when he was ready to cross the Schuylkill while General Anthony Wayne with 1,500 men and four guns was bivouacking in his rear, with a view to detaining him until help should arrive, it was the intelligence brought in by Loyalists that enabled the British commander in chief to surprise and cut off Wayne's men and so cross over without interruption. With the encamping of the invading host at Germantown and Philadelphia a few days later, both places became centers of attraction for adherents of the Crown from the surrounding region, and also from remoter parts of the country. On September 28th Howe issued a proclamation from his headquarters at Germantown, promising protection and security to all coming in and conducting themselves in accordance with his proclamation of a month earlier. Then, on October 8th, he announced

---

[4] *Pa. Mag. of Hist. and Biog.*, Oct., 1889, 298; Oct., 1885, 293, 294; Duane, ed., *Extracts from the Diary of Christopher Marshall*, 132; Sargent, ed., *Loyal Verses of Joseph Stansbury and Dr. Jonathan Odell*, 140; Scharf and Westcott, *Hist. of Phila.*, I, 350.

free pardon to all deserters who would voluntarily surrender before December 1st; and at the same time he published another proclamation in which he predicted the early suppression of the unnatural rebellion, and offered the inhabitants an opportunity to "coöperate in relieving themselves from the miseries attendant on tyranny and anarchy, and in restoring peace and good order with just and lawful authority." A bounty of fifty acres of vacant land for each private and of two hundred acres for each non-commissioned officer was promised to those who would enlist in the Provincial corps for two years or during the war. The Queen's Rangers were with the main army at Germantown, occupying the extreme right of the encampment, and probably the Royal Guides and Pioneers were near by; but on October 12th and 14th, respectively, Howe had the satisfaction of approving lists of officers for two additional Tory regiments, namely, the first battalion of the Pennsylvania Loyalists and the Roman Catholic Volunteers. Alfred Clifton was the commanding officer of the latter and William Allen of the former. Meantime, Tories were arriving at Germantown, including John Parrock and Alexander Kidd from Philadelphia, James Oram from the country near by, and Walter Willet from Bucks County. On October 19th Howe and his command transferred their camp to the Quaker City, and five days thereafter he designated the staff for the first battalion of the Maryland Loyalists at the instance of James Chalmers, its lieutenant colonel, who had previously been a resident of Philadelphia. On November 7th he did the same for the Philadelphia Light Dragoons, which was to consist of two companies with Richard Hovenden and Jacob James as captains. By November 26th, the Pennsylvania Loyalists numbered 145 men and the Maryland Loyalists 133. The first muster of the Roman Catholic Volunteers was taken on December 14th, and showed 62 men, but this number was nearly trebled during the next ten days (i.e., it reached 176 men on December 24th). Hovenden raised his troop of Dragoons in Philadelphia during November and December; while James recruited his troop in Chester County in the following January, the maximum number of the combined troops amounting to 109 men. The Bucks County Light Dragoons were recruited by Captain Thomas Sandford in Bucks County in the fall of 1777, and were commanded by Lieutenant Colonel Watson through the following winter and spring, while Sandford was a prisoner with the Americans. Its maximum enrollment was 55 men. In May, 1778, these three troops were organized into a squadron under Watson's command. During the time that the Bucks County corps was forming, Lieutenant Colonel John Van Dyke of Somerset County, N. J., was raising the West Jersey Volunteers in the southern counties of that Province. In January, 1778, he had 186 infantrymen, and during the course of the next four months he added 157 cavalrymen. Colonel Lord Rawdon, who had come to Philadelphia with the British, was enlisting the Volunteers of Ireland in the early part of May, and probably had 300 recruits before the city was evacuated. We should not overlook the accessions to the New Jersey Volunteers, Queen's Rangers, and the Royal Guides and Pioneers during this period of Tory enlistments: at least a few men joined the Guides and Pioneers, and about 225, if not more, were enrolled in the Rangers, including Captain John Ferdinand Dalziel Smyth and Lieutenant James Murray, with their 61 recruits. Smyth's commission as "an additional captain of the Rangers" was dated September 6, 1777. Many of the men who entered the ranks of this corps at the time of which we are speaking were refugees from Virginia and other Southern Colonies. It will be recalled that a number of recruits from Philadelphia joined the New Jersey Volunteers at Staten Island about the time the test was being applied in 1777. It was less than three months later, or when Cornwallis and his division entered Philadelphia, that the first and second battalions of this corps arrived there. Many volunteers at once enrolled themselves in the companies of Captains Thomas Colden and Norman McLeod; while two new companies were organized during November and December, 1777, one by Captain Donald Campbell and the other, which consisted of Cumberland men, by Captain Richard Cayford.

If now we attempt to figure the number of enlistments gained by the British from the invaded region, we get a total of between 1,700 and 1,800 men, a number that would be reduced to about 1,400, if we exclude the West Jersey Volunteers, who were not recruited in eastern Pennsylvania. Doubtless, this number should be still further reduced on account of accessions gained by detachments during raids into New Jersey. These figures do not agree with those of Joseph Galloway, who confines his to the enlistments secured in Philadelphia. In his testimony before Parliament, Galloway stated that there were within the lines at Philadelphia, when Howe occupied the city, 4,481 males capable of bearing arms, of whom a fourth were Quakers. His fourth is a generous one, however, leaving a remainder of 3,000. Of these, he says, Howe got only 974 men in all, who were chiefly deserters on account of the unpopularity of the Loyalists authorized to recruit. Galloway added that during Howe's occupation 2,300 deserters came in from the Continental army and were registered and qualified, besides 700 or 800 more, who never reported. Galloway's characterization of the men whom Howe commissioned to raise Provincial companies and battalions was certainly unjust: they were influential, but the British commander in chief lacked the power of infusing his subordinates with the proper military spirit. General Howe achieved great personal popularity among his men, but he achieved little else. Galloway was himself the chosen adviser of Howe, and as the virtual governor of Philadelphia during the occupation was active and serviceable in many ways; and yet he, like his chief, brought nothing of consequence to pass, not even good order in the city.[5]

After the occupation of Philadelphia, one of Mr. Galloway's first duties appears to have been to number all the inhabitants, in order to distinguish the loyal from the disaffected. In connection with the quartering of troops, he was able to show consideration for his old friends, even if he was not disposed to "lessen the distress of old enemies." He secured horses for the army, procured intelligence of the movements of the enemy through the agency of about eighty spies, rendered the capture of Mud Island Fort more speedy by the erection of some batteries, compiled a chart of all the roads in the vicinity of Philadelphia, and was assigned to administer the oaths of allegiance to inhabitants under Howe's proclamation. As this last named task was beyond his time and strength, Mr. Galloway had Enoch Story commissioned to perform it, and then had to ask for a day or two's extension of time beyond the two months originally announced, on account of the numbers crowding in on Mr. Story late in October. On December 4th, Mr. Galloway

---

[5] Scharf and Westcott, *Hist. of Phila.*, I, 349, 350, 352, 354, 360; *Pa. Mag. of Hist. and Biog.*, Oct., 1885. 291: Oct., 1889. 298: Jan., 1886. 429: Jan., 1910. 1: *2d Rep., Bur. of Archives, Ont.* (1904), Pt. I, 669, 684; II, 835, 741; *Am. Mss. in the Roy. Inst. of Gt. Brit.*, I, 136, 138, 139, 143, 150; Rev. W. O. Raymond's Ms. Notes from the Muster Rolls of Col. Edward Winslow; Stryker, *N. J. (Loyalist) Vols. in the Rev. War* (pamphlet), 12; Sabine, *Loyalists of the Am. Rev.*, II, 378; Siebert, "Refugee Loyalists of Conn." in *Trans. Roy. Soc. of Can.*, Ser. III, Vol. X (1916), 82, 83; Scott, *John Graves Simcoe*, 24; Read, *Life and Times of Governor Simcoe*, 27; *Rep. on Am. Mss. in the Roy. Inst. of Gt. Brit.*, I, 234; III, 170; IV, 474.

was appointed superintendent general of the police in the city and its environs and superintendent of imports and exports. He thus became the civil governor of Philadelphia, being vested with the administration of municipal affairs under the direction of General Howe. Mr. Story and Andrew Smith served as deputy officials of the port and Samuel Shoemaker, John Potts, and Daniel Coxe as magistrates of the police. Mr. Coxe was a noted refugee from New Jersey and had served in the King's Council of that Colony. Messrs. Potts and Shoemaker were well-known Philadelphians and former office-holders. Howe also appointed George Roberts, James Reynolds, James Sparks, and Joseph Stansbury for the city, together with John Hart for Southwark, and Francis Jeyes for the Northern Liberties, to be commissioners for selecting and supervising the night-watch, which numbered one hundred men in the city and ten each in the Northern Liberties and Southwark. Mr. Stansbury was a writer of Tory songs and verses and was later named as manager of a lottery for the relief of the poor. The preservation of peace and order was a difficult task, which subjected Mr. Galloway and the magistrates of the police to "extraordinary trouble and attention to business." These officials were therefore granted £25 sterling every quarter, in addition to their respective salaries. As Howe summarized the amounts paid to Mr. Galloway, they comprised an initial salary of £200 a year, £300 a year more as police magistrate, with 6s per diem for his clerk, and 20s per diem as superintendent of the port, or a total of £770 a year. Other local Loyalists rendered various other services. Thus, for example, George Harding of Philadelphia was employed in disarming those who were disaffected to the Crown and in finding proper locations for the troops. He was also authorized, along with twenty other men, to apprehend spies in the Continental service. Abraham Carlisle, another resident, was given oversight of the entrances to the city, with the power to issue passports. John Parrock, also of Philadelphia, supplied lumber from his wharves for the army quarters and for the navy. William Caldwell of Union Township was one of Galloway's secret service men, as well as a guide for several detachments of the troops. Joseph Murell rendered similar services. Gideon Vernon of Chester County carried dispatches for

General Howe and made observations among the enemy's forces, and Henry Hugh Ferguson was commissary of prisoners.[6]

It fell to Mr. Galloway, among his numerous duties, to regulate the markets, including the terms of buying and selling. Permits were required for dealers selling more than a bushel of salt or a hogshead of molasses to individual buyers, and this was also true in the case of those handling drugs in quantity. The purchaser of rum and spirits must buy from the importer only, but not more than a hogshead nor less than ten gallons at a time. Tavern licenses were also issued by Galloway, who granted permits to many refugee Loyalists to reopen deserted inns. As a swarm of strangers and fugitive Philadelphians arrived with the new *régime*, not a few seized the earliest opportunity of opening places for trade, including many shops and stores formerly kept by Whigs who were now absent. Christopher Marshall at Lancaster heard that there were about 120 new stores in Philadelphia, one kept by an Englishmen, another by an Irishman, "the remainder being 118 Scotchmen or Tories from Virginia." Joseph Stansbury became a dealer in china, William Drewitt Smith reopened his drug store after his return from Winchester, "James McDowell took Gilbert Barclay's store on Second Street, Bird's London Store supplanted Mrs. Devine's, George Leyburn ensconced himself in Francis Tilghman's store, William Robb sold merchandise where William Redwood had served his customers, Ninian Mangies took Thomas Gilpin's place, John Brander, Isaac Cox's, [and] Thomas Blane succeeded to Mease and Caldwell." These and other tradesmen of the city preferred solid coin in place of paper money under the new regulations, and so furnished Joseph Stansbury with a topic for one of his rhymed satires, in which he represented that the shop-keepers rejected the notes because they were issued against lands and mortgages held by the rebels, but that nevertheless many of the friends of government in town—

> "Sold each half-joe for twelve pounds Congress trash,
> Which purchased six pounds of this legal cash;
> Whereby they have, if you will bar the bubble,
> Instead of losing, made their money double."

[6] *Pa. Mag. of Hist. and Biog.*, Dec., 1902, 435, 436; Jan., 1886, 438; Scharf and Westcott, *Hist. of Phila.*, I, 360; 2d Rep., *Bur. of Archives, Ont.* (1904), Pt. I, 109, 112, 129, 160, 165, 222, 260, 269, 296, 498, 517, 564, 669, 684; II, 741, 827, 835; Sabine, *Loyalists of the Am. Rev.*, I, 296, 339, 421; II, 112, 199, 301, 325; *Rep. on Am. Mss. in the Roy. Inst. of Gt. Brit.*, I, 145, 160, 201, 218, 277, 364.

Among these friends of government were several publishers of Tory newspapers. Until Howe's arrival in Philadelphia, Benjamin Towne's *Pennsylvania Evening Post* had been Whig in politics. Then, it abruptly became Tory, only to change back again with the return of the Americans. James Humphreys revived the *Pennsylvania Ledger* during the British and Loyalist supremacy, using the royal arms for the heading of his paper; and the *Pennsylvania Gazette* also sought the patronage of the military and refugee populace during the same period. These last two publications suspended about May 23, 1778.[7]

The Tories in Philadelphia were panic-stricken by the battle of Germantown, which was fought October 5, 1777; and some of them moved out of the city, though probably not for long. As the wounded were brought into Philadelphia for care in numerous improvised hospitals, the resident Quakers could not avoid seeing more or less of the cruelties of actual warfare; and two days after the battle they sent a deputation to Howe and thence to Washington with testimonies on the ungodliness of war. In their communication to the latter, they made use of the opportunity to assert the innocence of themselves and of their Society of imputations cast upon them; to explain that the aim of their body was to seek only for peace and righteousness in the world, with equal love to all men, and to intimate their desire for Washington's aid in behalf of their brethren still in exile at Winchester, Va. The raising of this last question inclined the American commander in chief to send his callers to Lancaster to lay their request respecting the exiles before the Supreme Executive Council and Congress; but as they timidly withdrew their suggestion, he relieved their minds by inviting them to dinner and ordering them, as one of his officers expressed it, "only to do pennance a few days at Pott's-grove." [8]

From the time the British first entered Philadelphia, September 26, 1777, until they left it, June 17, 1778, or during a period of eight and a half months, fugitives were coming in singly and in groups, as opportunity offered, from the neighboring country, including all the counties of eastern Pennsylvania from Northampton and Bucks on the north to Lancaster and York on the west of the metropolis. They came in also in considerable numbers from

---

[7] Scharf and Westcott, *Hist. of Phila.*, I, 359, 366, 367, 383; Sabine, *Loyalists of the Am. Rev.*, II, 360; I, 554, 555.
[8] Scharf and Westcott, *Hist. of Phila.*, I, 359.

Virginia, Maryland, and especially from New Jersey. James Allen, who sent his family into the city in January, 1778, and followed with his sister, Mrs. John Penn, on February 13, noted in his *Diary* after his arrival that the town was filled with refugees from the country, and that the Tories of many localities in Bucks County and in New Jersey had risen against severe persecution and brought in their oppressors as prisoners. In neighborhoods where the number of Loyalists was too small to accomplish such feats of valor, the approach of a detachment of British troops or of a rescue party from the seat of the army had to be awaited. An appeal for succor from a group of Jerseymen was responded to by twenty West Jersey refugees, who crossed to the east side of the Delaware from Philadelphia, had a skirmish with a band of watchful Americans at the mouth of Mantua Creek, and returned with their rescued friends, February 3d. At the end of this month, it was reported in the *Pennsylvania Evening Post* that large numbers of Jerseymen had joined a detachment of the army since its arrival in their vicinity. The *Pennsylvania Ledger* of March 18th declared that there was not a day on which "great numbers" of Loyalists were not flocking to the city, being "driven by the most obdurate and merciless tyranny from all that is dear and valuable in life." An item of May 11th in Allen's *Diary* stated that the "persecutions in the country were very great, that those who refused to subscribe to the test in the various Provinces were treated as enemies and suffered confiscation of their estates, and that Philadelphia was swarming with refugees."[9]

While, as we have already seen, a few of these unfortunate people had sufficient resources still at command to enable them to engage in business, and others received official positions in the city to which salaries were attached, the great majority of the refugees must have been under the necessity of depending on the army or the city authorities for their housing and support. It will be shown farther on that those Loyalists who were embodied in regiments were employed in patrolling the country roads so as to enable farmers and gardeners to reach the city market with their produce, and that they also secured quantities of booty through foraging and plundering expeditions; but in view of the pressing needs of the raiders themselves and of the regular troops, it may be doubted

[9] *Pa. Mag. of Hist. and Biog.*, Jan., 1886, 431, 436; *N. J. Archives*, 2d Ser., II, 35, 65, 81, 126, 127.

whether or not any of these extra supplies ever reached those refugees who were too impoverished to supply their own wants through the ordinary channels of trade. According to the census that Howe had taken shortly after his entry into Philadelphia, the population amounted to a little more than 23,700, of which the females numbered 13,403, not to mention the children, of whom there were certainly many, although we get no figures concerning them. We can thus see that the proportion of dependents was extremely large, and we know that it was being constantly increased by the arrival of distressed Loyalists. It is easy to understand, therefore, why in the winter of 1777-78, Howe sanctioned the collection of contributions for the support of the almshouse, thirty-two collectors being appointed for the purpose; why as spring approached the commander in chief exhorted the Loyalists in one of his proclamations "to exert themselves in raising vegetables" and other things for the use of the soldiers and inhabitants, and why in April he authorized a lottery, which was placed under the management of Stephen Shewell, James Craig, Reynold Keene, Joseph Stansbury, and twelve others. This lottery produced £1,012 10s for the benefit of the poor in the city.[10] But the best efforts of the Loyalists to supply garden and farm produce for the army and the multitude of refugees within the lines were quite inadequate to relieve a situation which James Allen, writing on June 8, vividly described in the following words: "For 7 months Gen Washington with an army not exceeding 7 or 8000 men has lain at Valley Forge 20 miles from here, unmolested; while Sr W. Howe with more than double his number & the best troops in the world, has been shut up in Philada, where the markets are extravagantly high, & parties of the enemy all round the city within a mile or two robbing the market people. Consequently the distress of the citizens and particularly the Refugees has been very great."

During the winter and spring of 1777 and 1778, the Philadelphia Light Dragoons had been coöperating with the Queen's Rangers in securing the country and facilitating the inhabitants in bringing their produce into Philadelphia. The Rangers, with Redoubt No. 1 at Kensington as their headquarters, patrolled the roads above, particularly the Frankford road, to enable the Bucks County farmers to drive into town with the products of their farms

---

and dairies. The market people, however, were prevented by the Americans from coming down below Frankford, and their light horse made frequent sallies on the Rangers' quarters at Kensington. In December or January the withdrawal by Brigadier General Lacey of some of his Pennsylvania militia from the posts they had been occupying in the Delaware-Schuylkill peninsula enabled the patrolling Tory regiments to forage and ravage at will. On February 14th, Hovenden's troop of Philadelphia Light Dragoons went up the Bristol road, and Captain Evan Thomas with his Bucks County Volunteers took the Bustleton road. On their return they brought back most of the officials of Bucks County. During the same month they made other forays into the County of Bucks, as the result of which they captured a number of Continental soldiers, a quantity of cloth greatly needed by Washington's army at Valley Forge, and a drove of 130 cattle. About a month later the Queen's Rangers, the New Jersey Volunteers, and other troops to the number of about 1,500 men engaged in foraging expeditions into New Jersey and Cumberland County, Pa. When, at length, the Pennsylvania militia under Brigadier General Lacey was strengthened, the farmers of Bucks County found it more difficult to reach the Philadelphia market. Many of them were captured, and some were condemned by court-martial to be hanged. Later, those caught conveying produce to the British were deprived of their teams and laden wagons, and were in many cases subjected to a flogging. Lacey's operations were now so successful in cutting off supplies from the city that on May 1, 1778, the Queen's Rangers, the Philadelphia Light Dragoons, and other regiments were dispatched to destroy the energetic officer and his command. Taken by surprise, twenty-six of the Americans were killed, and some of the prisoners and wounded were put to death in brutal ways by their Tory captors.[11]

The civil authorities, as well as the military, sought to suppress the intercourse between Philadelphia and the outside world during the period of the British occupation of the city. On October 12, 1777, a new "supplement" to the test act of four months earlier was passed, because the latter had not been found satisfactory in actual experience. The supplement was framed to stop the passing from county to county of male white non-jurors and Loyalists, and

---

[11] *Pa. Mag. of Hist. and Biog.*, Jan., 1886, 438; Scharf and Westcott, *Hist. of Phila.*, I, 360, 361, 365, 373, 374, 375.

especially of those coming out of Philadelphia, which was now in the possession of the British. The age limit of those who were ordered to subscribe to the oath or affirmation was now reduced from eighteen to sixteen years, and justices of the peace were empowered not only to exact the oath, but also to require such further security as they might think necessary in individual cases. Imprisonment without bail was the alternative, the end of the sentence depending on the willingness of the suspect to subscribe and furnish the extra security. The final section of the law made it possible for one or more sworn accusers to have persons who avoided traveling about brought before a justice on suspicion of unfriendliness to the independence of the United States, in order that the test might be applied to him. This measure was to go into operation three days after its enactment. The new Council of Safety (October 21 to December 6, 1777) and after it the Supreme Executive Council in their sessions at Lancaster tried and sentenced many offenders on the charge of supplying the royal troops with provisions, or of prosecuting an illicit trade with them. The usual penalty inflicted was one month's imprisonment at hard labor, although in certain instances the term of incarceration was lengthened to that of the war, and occasionally fifty or one hundred lashes were added for some special reason, such as the passing of counterfeit Continental currency by the culprit. As some of those carrying on the forbidden trade lived on the east side of the Delaware River, the civil authorities of New Jersey also employed repressive measures. The General Assembly of that State passed a bill which was intended to prevent all communication between the parties concerned; but since the act was not well enforced, the magistrates of Burlington County, N. J., announced their determination on February 16, 1778, to execute it in the most rigorous manner. On the same date, the governor of New Jersey, William Livingston, recommended the enactment of a bill authorizing the militia, or any other persons, to seize all effects suspected of being carried to or from the enemy, the seized goods to be appropriated to those taking them, in case the persons thus dispossessed should be found guilty by legal process.[12]

These efforts to terminate the intercourse between Philadelphia and the outside world served in considerable measure to increase the distress already existing among the refugees

---

[12] *Laws of Pa.*, II, 159; *N. J. Archives*, 2d. Ser., II, 56, 57, 87.

and inhabitants of the city, already greatly aggravated, it
may be added, by the exorbitant prices of provisions and merchandise prevailing there. Notwithstanding these unfortunate conditions, however, there was no dearth of festivities among the men
of the camps and the social set in the metropolis during the Tory
supremacy. When off duty the soldiers gave themselves up to
amusements. The officers formed themselves into dining clubs,
among which was the "Loyal Association Club"; they also held
cricket matches, and patronized a cock-pit where mains were
fought for a hundred guineas. Weekly balls from the end of January to that of April afforded ample opportunity for the young
ladies of the Tory set to establish social relations with the military gentlemen in town. The old South Street Theatre witnessed
a series of plays, in some of which the officers took part. Howe
paid the price of all this unwarranted gaiety, as well as of his
supineness in martial affairs, by being supplanted in his
command. On May 7, Sir Henry Clinton landed at Billingsport,
and the next day he arrived in Philadelphia. Before Howe
embarked for England, he was complimented by a regatta
on the Delaware and a pageant of knights, squires, and
ladies on the beautiful grounds of the Wharton mansion
at Walnut Grove. This combined celebration, which was
planned and chiefly managed by Major John André, and was widely
heralded as the *Meschianza*, occurred, May 18th, and was participated in by many of the Loyalist belles of the city. The day
ended with a grand ball, which lasted until after sunrise the next
morning. This concluding event, however, was disturbed by an
attack on the abatis north of town by Captain McLane and a detachment of Americans. About the same time, Howe learned that
Lafayette and 2,500 of the enemy had crossed the Schuylkill and
encamped some distance below Marston's Ford. He, therefore,
craved the distinction of closing his term of service with the capture of Lafayette and his force. Although he and Clinton led out
11,000 men in the effort to attain this object, the French general
and his men succeeded in recrossing the river, with but a slight
loss at the ford. Having thus failed to redeem his military reputa-
tion, General Howe relinquished the command of the army to
Clinton, and sailed for England, May 24, 1778.[13]

---

[13] Scharf and Westcott, *Hist. of Phila.*, I, 371-382; *Gentleman's Magazine*, Aug., 1778.

On the same day the new commander in chief held a council of war, which decided in favor of evacuating the city; and this decision seems to have been communicated to a meeting of "gentlemen, merchants, and citizens" that took place at the British Tavern. The local historian, Westcott, says that notice had been previously given that all deserters from the American army who wished to go to England would be sent, and that "many availed themselves of the privilege." Probably, the news of the intended evacuation did not come as an entire surprise to the community, for Mrs. Drinker recorded in her *Journal*, under date of May 23d, that preparations for the departure were being made by "many of the inhabitants." On June 3d three regiments crossed the Delaware and encamped near Cooper's Ferry and Gloucester. Two days later Captain Johann Heinrichs of the Hessian Jager Corps, who was then at the Neck near the city, wrote to his brother that "about one thousand royally inclined families" in Philadelphia were "willing to leave hearth and home and with their chattels go with the army." A few days later still the British Peace Commissioners arrived in the city; and one of them, Lord Carlisle, wrote that he found everything in confusion, "the army upon the point of leaving town, and about three thousand of the miserable inhabitants embarked on board our ships, to convey them from a place where they thought they would receive no mercy from those who will take possession after us." In a letter of June 15th to the colonial secretary in London, the Commissioners stated that they had found the greater part of those who had put themselves under the King's protection either retiring on board ships in the Delaware River, or endeavoring to effect their reconciliation with Congress by hastening to take the oath of allegiance to the Confederated States of America within the allotted time, in order to save their property from confiscation and themselves from "the violent resentment of an exulting and unrestrained enemy." As the time for taking the oath of allegiance had already been extended to June 1, 1778, it is highly improbable that additional days of grace were granted to those seeking to make amends for such obvious reasons. Nevertheless, a good many whose past conduct identified them as undesirable citizens in the eyes of the Whigs chose to remain, as did also the wives and children of some undoubted Loyalists who left with the troops, or had taken their departure earlier. In these closing days of the British occupation, Mrs. Drinker records the parting calls of Enoch Story and Richard Waln, and remarks that Samuel Shoemaker and many other inhabitants had gone on board the vessels. Clinton's intention had been to send his troops back to New York by sea, as they had come; but instead he filled the waiting fleet with Tory families and ordered his army to take up the line of march across the Jerseys.[14]

The van of the army withdrew from Philadelphia, June 17th, the main body following on the next day. With the retiring troops marched the Loyalist regiments which had been formed during the British occupation of the city, as well as those which had come as part of the invading host. Since many of the local refugees attempted to carry with them more or less of their possessions, and in some cases the appropriated property of absent Whigs, they impeded the movements of the troops; and according to an item in the *Pennsylvania Evening Post* of June 20th, some of the fugitives, along with other prisoners, were captured by a pursuing body of American light horse. By the time Allentown, N. J., was reached, the Queen's Rangers had been joined by many new refugees, who supplied the guides needed for the remainder of the march. Near Monmouth Court House strong detachments of the American army, which had been sent forward by Washington, attacked the British, June 28th, killing over 250 officers and men and wounding many more, including Lieutenant Colonel Simcoe and Captain Stephenson of the Rangers. While Clinton's force was experiencing these difficulties, the British fleet was reported in Philadelphia to have lost several transports to the enemy, on one of which were five refugee families with their effects. From Monmouth the Queen's Rangers led the way to Sandy Hook, where on July 5th the embarkation of the troops for the brief passage to New York began. They left behind them in New Jersey at least two Tory battalions, namely, the Volunteers of Ireland and the West Jersey Regiment. At the close of August, 1778, the former corps was stationed at Six Mile Hill, a few miles to the southeast of New Brunswick, while the latter was then at Sandy Hook. Towards the end of the following February the Volunteers of Ireland were at New York, with a strength of 509 men. At least two companies of the West Jersey

---

[14] Scharf and Westcott, *Hist. of Phila.*, I, 383, 384; *Pa. Mag. of Hist. and Biog.*, Oct., 1889, 307; XXII (1898), 145.

Regiment, if not the entire corps, had by this time been incorporated with the New Jersey Volunteers on Staten Island.[15]

After Clinton's army landed at New York City the various Loyalist regiments, which had accompanied it, were distributed among the British posts of the neighborhood. Thus, by July 15, 1778, the Queen's Rangers were encamped at King's Bridge, where they were soon joined by the Philadelphia Light Dragoons and the Bucks County Light Dragoons, the three together numbering 448 men at the end of August. The Pennsylvania Loyalists had been sent at the same time to New Utrecht, L. I., near Brooklyn; while the Roman Catholic Volunteers and the Maryland Loyalists had been assigned to Flushing Fly, a few miles to the northeast. Of the three corps last named the August muster showed that the first had 188 men, the second 331, and the third 171. At the close of February, 1779, the Volunteers of Ireland, with a strength of 509 men, were at New York, and the Royal Guides and Pioneers, numbering 173 men, were also there and thereabouts.[16]

During the British occupation of Philadelphia the town suffered from spoliation and destruction of property to such an extent that, when the Americans returned to it, they found it in a wretched condition. Nor was this havoc confined to the estates of the absent Whigs. Robert Morton, the Loyalist, says in his *Diary* that the British set fire to "the Fairhill mansion house, Jonathan Mifflin's, and many others, amounting to eleven, besides outhouses, barns, etc.," on November 22d. All these were the buildings of Loyalists, and were only part of the structures similarly dealt with in the same neighborhood, where eighteen other homes were deliberately burned, the reason assigned—according to Morton—being that the Americans had been shooting at the British pickets from these houses. Mrs. Deborah Logan, who witnessed this incendiarism, "counted seventeen fires" from the roof of her mother's house on Chestnut Street. Pierre Du Simitiere, a resident of Philadelphia during this period, wrote that it would be in vain to attempt to give an account of the devastation committed by those in possession indiscriminately on Whig and Tory prop-

---

[15] Siebert, *The Flight of the Am. Loyalists to the Brit. Isles* (pamphlet), 8, 9, and the references there given; Scott, *John Graves Simcoe*, 22; Reed, *The Life and Times of Simcoe*, 29; *N. J. Archives*, 2d Ser., II, 263, 264, 267, 269, 272-276, 285-291, 296; *Simcoe's Journal*, 62 *passim*; Ms. Muster Rolls of Col. Edward Winslow (in possession of the N. B. Hist. Soc., St. John, N. B.)

[16] Rev. W. O. Raymond's Ms. Notes from Col. Edward Winslow's Muster Rolls.

erty in the environs of the city. He added that "the persecution that numbers of worthy citizens underwent from the malice of the Tories; the tyranny of the police on all those they supposed to be the friends of the liberties of America; all these would fill a volume." Entries in Christopher Marshall's *Remembrancer* from June 23d to June 26th, inclusive, confirm these earlier testimonies: they speak of the houses ruined and destroyed within a mile or two of the city and of "the desolation with the dirt, filth, stench, and flies in and about the town" as scarcely credible. Marshall writes that he was struck with wonder and amazement at the "scenes of malice and wanton cruelty," but that his late dwelling-house was not so bad as many others, although it was "quite gone," its roof, doors, windows, etc., being "either destroyed or carried away entirely." It was not until 1782 that an appraisement was made of all these damages, in accordance with an act of the General Assembly. It then appeared that the loss sustained by the inhabitants of Philadelphia amounted to £187,280 5s. According to this appraisement, forty-six persons suffered damages exceeding one thousand pounds, the losses of eight of these ranging from £3,000 up to £5,622. As Germantown had suffered during the early days of the occupation, having been the headquarters of the main army under Howe and the scene of a battle, it was included in the appraisment. Its claims numbered 137, although some of its losses were not included in this list.[17]

---

[17] *Statutes at Large of Pa.*, IX, 145-151; *Laws of Pa.*, II, 389; Scharf and Westcott, *Hist. of Phila.*, I, 367, 384, 386.

CHAPTER V

WHIG REPRISALS UPON SOME OF THE LOYALISTS DURING AND AFTER THE BRITISH OCCUPATION OF PHILADELPHIA

It was not until more than a fortnight after the British had occupied Philadelphia, and only a few days after Howe had offered bounties of land to such Loyalists as would enlist, that a new Council of Safety was constituted by an act of the General Assembly, October 13, 1777. This new council, which comprised the members of the Supreme Executive Council and nine other gentlemen, was vested with full power to provide for the preservation of the Commonwealth by such ordinances as it deemed necessary, and to punish capitally or otherwise all persons guilty of transgressing these ordinances or the laws of the State previously enacted. This part of the new law was directed against those considered to be inimical to the common cause of liberty. Another section authorized the seizure of provisions and other necessaries for the American army and the inhabitants of the State. The duration of these powers was limited, however, to the end of the next meeting of the Assembly. On October 21st the Council of Safety began to operate under this measure by ordaining the collection of arms and accoutrements and shoes and stockings from such inhabitants of Chester County as had failed to take the oaths of allegiance and abjuration required by a law of February 11th in the same year. At the same time it passed an ordinance naming commissioners for the City of Philadelphia and the eleven counties of the State, who were to seize the personal estates and effects of all inhabitants then or in the future guilty of abandoning their families or habitations and joining the King's army, or resorting to any place in its possession within the Commonwealth and supplying the royal troops with provisions, intelligence, or other aid. The commissioners were to make an inventory of the property seized, dispose of the perishable part, and keep safely the money and goods taken, subject to future disposition by the Legislature. The Council justified its action by declaring that divers persons had renounced their allegiance to the State and, wickedly joining themselves to the enemy, had afforded assistance thereto in various ways, and it further declared that it was repugnant to the practice of all nations to protect and preserve the property of their avowed foes.[1]

An ordinance passed a little later authorized the collection of sums from delinquents, of whom there were many in the State, who were indebted to the public treasury for advances paid to their substitutes in the militia, the collection being enforcible by the distress and sale of the goods and chattels of such as refused or neglected to pay. This regulation was soon followed by another requiring the seizure of arms and accoutrements, blankets, and other supplies for the American army from all inhabitants who had not yet taken the oaths of allegiance and abjuration. On December 6th the powers granted to the Council of Safety were terminated by proclamation of the Supreme Executive Council, these powers having been in force less than two months.[2]

In the early months of the following year the Assembly at Lancaster supplemented the confiscatory measures of the Council of Safety by legislation which was directed against the college in Philadelphia and against persons associating with the enemy. Among such persons were several trustees of the college, while the name of the Reverend William Smith, D.D., the provost of the institution, had been included in a list of individuals considered to be dangerous to the State, which had been drawn up in the previous September. Since, therefore, the college had come to be generally regarded as a Tory institution and was, moreover, in the enemy's hands, the Assembly passed an act, January 2, 1778, by whch the authority of the trustees of the college and academy was suspended for a limited time. An act for "the attainder of divers Traitors" was also passed (March 6), which provided that if certain persons failed to appear by a specified date (April 20th), their estates would become vested in the Commonwealth. Those designated were Joseph Galloway, Andrew Allen and his brothers John and William, the Reverend Jacob Duché, and Samuel Shoemaker, all of Philadelphia: John Potts of Philadelphia County, James Rankin of York, Gilbert Hicks of Bucks, Nathaniel Vernon of Chester, Christian Foutz of Lancaster, and Reynold Keene and John Biddle of Berks. Provision was made for the discovery and seizure of the

---

[1] *Col. Records of Pa.*, XI, 325, 326, 328, 329.
[2] *Ibid.*, 332, 333, 339, 363.

estates of these persons, as also for the attainting of other individuals adhering to the enemy. Indeed, the act declared that all subjects and inhabitants of the State who should at any time during the war voluntarily serve the King, either by land or sea in an official or private capacity, would *ipso facto* become attainted of high treason, and debtors of traitors were ordered to pay their obligations to the Supreme Executive Council, instead of to the proscribed. In accordance with this law, eight different proclamations were issued by the Council against persons designated as traitors during a period which included the years from 1778 to 1781. The number of those thus published were thirteen in the first proclamation (March 6th, 1778), fifty-seven in the second (May 8th), seventy-five in the third (May 21st), two hundred in the fourth (June 15th), and sixty-two in the fifth (October 30th), or a total of 407 during the year 1778. The proclamation of June 22, 1779, named thirty; that of October 3, 1780, ten; that of March 20, 1781, fifteen; and the last, which was dated April 27, 1781, designated one only. Thus, the number of persons announced as traitors in the entire series of proclamations for being reported as having joined the British was only 453, of which 109 were former inhabitants of Philadelphia, seventy-six of Philadelphia County, seventy-seven of Bucks, eighty-seven of Chester, nine of York, thirty-five of Northampton, four of Bedford, three of Trenton, N. J., and one each of the States of Maryland and New York. As this total was not more than ten percent of the number of Loyalists who left Philadelphia at the evacuation, not to mention the numerous refugees whom we know to have fled from the State during the preceding years, it will be seen that the Council of Safety might have been far more drastic than it was in applying the penalties of attainder and forfeiture of property to the adherents of the Crown.[3]

Among these attainted men all classes were represented: there were numbers of laborers, yeomen, and husbandmen; there were many also who had been engaged in shop-keeping and in a variety of trades; among the merchants we find Enoch and Thomas Story, Abel James, John and Charmless Hart, Matthias Aspden, Malcolm Ross, David Sproat, Oswald Eve, and Robert White; John Bray and Hugh Lindon were school-masters; among the attorneys

---

[3] *Colon. Records of Pa.*, XI, 483-485, 504, 505, 512-518, 587; XII, 27, 496, 665, 710; *Laws of Pa.*, II, 165-176; Scharf and Westcott, *Hist. of Phila.*, I, 377.

were Charles Stedman, Jr., Abel Evans, and Christian Hook; at least two prominent physicians were proscribed, namely, Anthony Yeldall and Andrew DeNormandie; William Drewitt Smith and Christian Voght, the latter of the Borough of Lancaster, were druggists; there were a few who were designated as "gentlemen," for example, Ross Curry, Alfred and William Clifton, John Kearsley, Jr., and John Young of Graeme Park; then there were some who had held high rank in civil and military circles, such as Joseph Galloway and Andrew Allen, "late members of the Congress of the thirteen United Colonies," the Reverend Jacob Duché, the first chaplain of Congress; John Biddle, collector of excise for the County of Berks and deputy quarter master general of the American army; Christian Foutz, lieutenant colonel of militia in Chester County, and Benedict Arnold, major general in the army of the United States; and finally there were numerous officials of minor rank, including Joseph Swanwick and John Bartlett of the Custom House of Philadelphia; John Smith, gauger of the port of the city; Samuel Carrigues, Sr., clerk of the market; William Austen, keeper of the New Jersey ferry; Abraham Iredell, surveyor; Nathaniel Vernon, sheriff of Chester County; Samuel Biles, sheriff of Bucks County; Robert Land, justice of the peace of Northampton County, and Samuel Shoemaker, alderman of Philadelphia.

On April 1, 1778, the Assembly had passed a law "for the Further Security of the Government," which extended the time for subscribing to the test to June 1st. Any male white inhabitant of eighteen years of age or older who failed to comply was to be incapable of bringing any legal action, serving as a guardian, executor, or administrator, receiving a legacy, or making a will, besides being subject to double taxes. Non-jurors might be imprisoned for three months, or they might be fined £10 or less and required to leave the State within thirty days, besides forfeiting their goods and chattels to the Commonwealth and their lands and tenements to the persons entitled by law to inherit them. As many individuals had been entering Philadelphia on various pretexts since its occupation by the British army, permits issuable by Congress, the Executive Council, or General Washington were to be required. The failure to observe this requirement laid the delinquent liable to a fine of £50 or less and imprisonment during the court's pleasure. The disabilities imposed upon non-jurors by the present law and the test acts of 1777 were to last for life. Office-holders under the proprietary government who did not renounce their allegiance to the Crown before June 1, 1778, or within ten days after returning to the State, were to have the privilege of selling their estates within ninety days, under permission from the Supreme Executive Council, and departing, or be deemed enemies and compelled to forfeit their goods and chattels, lands and tenements. Finally, all trustees, provosts, rectors, professors, and tutors of any college or academy, all school-masters, merchants, traders, lawyers, doctors, druggists, notaries, and clerks who did not submit to the test would thereby be disabled from following their vocations and, on conviction of disregarding this injunction, might be fined as much as £500. The object of this last section of the new test law was to enable the Supreme Executive Council to deal with the officers of the College, Academy, and Charitable School of the City of Philadelphia.[4]

It was not, however, until in February, 1779, that a resolution was adopted appointing a committee to investigate the early history, the purposes, and the condition of the college. In consonance with the wishes of the trustees, Provost Smith submitted a written defense of the course and conduct of the trustees and other officers, but without the desired effect; for on the 27th of the following November a law was passed by which the proprietary charters of the College, Academy, and Charitable School were "amended" and the provost and all others connected with these institutions were removed. The name of the college was changed to "The University of the State of Pennsylvania," and the rights and property hitherto vested in the trustees were transferred to a new board appointed by the Assembly, which also authorized the Supreme Executive Council to reserve a sufficient number of estates confiscated from attainted Loyalists, but as yet unsold, to endow the reorganized establishment with an annual income not to exceed £1,500. During the next few years the university was vested with sixty such estates. The annual rent charges which these properties would produce were carefully computed in bushels of wheat and totaled not far from 1,550 bushels. The estates thus appropriated for the university were scattered through five counties, twenty-one of them being in the City of Philadelphia, twenty-one others in the county of the same name, seven each in Berks and Chester counties, three in Bucks, and one in Lancaster. Five of the properties in Berks

---

[4] *Statutes at Large of Pa.*, IX, 149-151; Scharf and Westcott, *Hist. of Phila.*, I, 377.

County had belonged to Andrew Allen, and eight of those in Philadelphia had been held by John Parrock. Only two of the other estates had belonged to a single owner at the time of their confiscation. In addition to these sixty properties, the trustees, with the concurrence of the Supreme Executive Council, purchased fifteen other confiscated real estates at the public sales, all but three of these being in the City of Philadelphia. They also bought fifteen "rent charges, together with all the estate, interest and claim of the Commonwealth" in and to the lots and lands in the city from which these rentals emanated. Eleven of these last purchases had belonged to John Parrock and the other four to Samuel Shoemaker. Thus, by the purchase of the trustees and by the action of the Council, the university secured a total of ninety confiscated properties, of which forty-eight were located in Philadelphia and twenty-four in the county of the same name. As the income of these properties did not amount as yet to more than a yearly value of £1,381 5s 7½d, computing wheat at the rate of ten shillings per bushel, the Legislature proceeded on September 22, 1785, to enact that the "several confiscated estates, lands, tenements and heriditaments and rent charges" be fully and absolutely vested in and confirmed to the University of the State of Pennsylvania."[5]

Meantime, Thomas Mifflin and nine other trustees of the old college presented a memorial to the Council of Censors proposing to restore the original corporation. The committee to which this memorial was referred reported in favor of the action requested. The matter was also brought to the attention of the Assembly by a letter from the former provost, Dr. Smith, and the committee named to consider the question reported that the college had never forfeited its rights nor committed any offense against the laws. The committee, therefore, recommended a resolution for adoption repealing the act of November 27, 1779, by which the property and rights of the college had been transferred to the board named by the Assembly.

In accordance with these recommendations, the Assembly by a vote of twenty-eight yeas to twenty-five nays enacted a law, March 6, 1789, in the preamble of which the admission was frankly made that the corporation, trustees, professors, and other officers of the old college and its subsidiary schools had been deprived of their charters, franchises, and estates without trial by jury or

[5] *Laws of Pa.*, II, 223-229, 258; III, 113-121, 302-306.

proof of forfeiture. The new law therefore repealed such parts of the act of November 27, 1779, as concerned the ancient corporation, its charters, and its former rights, and provided for the reinstatement of the trustees and the restoration of the faculty to all of the rights, emoluments, and estates which they had formerly held and enjoyed, except such rents and profits as had been received by the board of the university before March 2, 1789, such sums as had already been paid out in the discharge of just debts and contracts, and such bonds and mortgages as had been transferred, cancelled, or paid by it. The trustees of the university were, however, to be accountable to the trustees of the college for the value of these mortgages and bonds. Inasmuch as the unrepealed sections of the law of 1779 left the university still intact and in possession of the confiscated estates with which it had been endowed, the effect of the act of 1789 was to make the college and the university separate institutions.[6]

For the next seven years the two institutions, both located in Philadelphia, sustained the relation of rivals in the educational field. Then, their respective boards addressed petitions to the Assembly, in which they set forth that they had agreed to certain terms of union in the desire that the two might be combined by legislative action. Accordingly, an act was passed, September 30, 1791, which provided that the name of the resulting institution should be "The University of Pennsylvania," the location remaining in the city; it also provided that the existing boards of trustees should elect twelve persons from among their own members on or before December 1st, who, with the governor of the State, should constitute a new board. This body was to have control of all funds, was to support a charity school for boys and another for girls, and was to choose the faculties in arts and medicine for the new university from each constituent institution equally. By this highly commendable action, the way was cleared for the future growth and usefulness of the University of Pennsylvania.[7]

Notwithstanding the fact that Governor John Penn had been deposed and the proprietary *régime* superseded since the summer of 1776, the Penns were left in a state of uncertainty for more than three years as to the settlement of their claims. In February, 1778, shortly after the Assembly had passed the act of attainder and

---

[6] *Laws of Pa.*, III, 302-306; Scharf and Westcott, *Hist. of Phila.*, I, 385, 386.
[7] *Statutes at Large of Pa.*, XIV, 184-187.

confiscation against Loyalists adhering to the enemy, it took up this highly important question. Governor Penn was notified at this time, and chose counsel to represent the family interests. Still, no action was taken until November 27, 1779, when after several days spent in discussion of the subject, the Assembly passed a law in which the proprietary charter was construed as an instrument "containing a public trust for the benefit of those who should settle in the State of Pennsylvania, coupled with a particular interest accruing to . . . . William Penn and his heirs, but in its very nature and essence subject and subordinate to the great and general purposes of society sanctioned in the said grant." The law further declared that the claims of the proprietaries to the whole of the soil bestowed by the charter, and likewise to the quit rents and purchase money for grants since made by them, were no longer consistent with the safety, liberty, and happiness of the inhabitants, who had rescued themselves and their possessions from the tyranny of Great Britain, and were then defending themselves from the inroads of the savages; and it asserted that effective measures were demanded by the great expenses of the war and by the daily emigration of "multitudes of inhabitants" to neighboring States, where lands were being located and settled. Accordingly, the new law decreed that the interest, title, and claim which the proprietaries possessed in the soil of the late Province on July 4, 1776, together with the royalties, lordships, and all other hereditaments authorized by the charter, were henceforth vested in the Commonwealth, and subject to division, appropriation, and conveyance, in accordance with such laws as might be later enacted. Exception was made, however, of the rights appertaining to other persons than the proprietaries, by virtue of any deeds, warrants, or surveys of grants derived from the Penns, and filed in the Land Office before the Declaration of Independence. That is to say, the law confirmed both the legal and equitable rights of such persons. To the proprietaries themselves it secured their private estates and inheritances, besides such manors or "proprietary tenths" as had been surveyed and reserved in the Land Office by July 4, 1776, and in addition the quit rents and other rents belonging to them. It was further provided that commissioners should be appointed to constitute a Board of Property, with power to collect all papers, records, maps, and surveys in the possession of the propietaries or their agents respecting the lands within the State, and with power also to grant patents, confirm titles, appoint surveyors and other officers, and receive money arising from the sale of lands not as yet surveyed or located.[8]

In compensation for the proprietary rights of which the Penns were deprived by the above provisions, and in "remebrance of the enterprising spirit" of the founder of the State and "of the expectations and dependence of his descendants," the law awarded the sum of £130,000 sterling to the devisees and legatees of Thomas Penn, in such proportions as should thereafter be fixed by the Legislature. Although a section of the law provided that no part of the sum stipulated should be paid within less than one year after the termination of the war, it was not until February 9, 1785, that an act was passed authorizing the immediate payment of £15,000 as the first annual instalment. This amount had not been fully paid, however, at the end of March, 1787. Meanwhile, interest was accruing on the residue of the debt. Hence, at this time (March 28th), it was enacted that the State treasurer pay the respective balances still due on the first instalment to John Penn, the elder, and John Penn, the younger, together with interest at six percent per annum from September 3, 1784, and the Supreme Executive Council was ordered to issue warrants on the treasurer forthwith for the discharge of the second and third instalments of £15,000 each, with interest from the dates of their maturity, respectively. Warrants or orders for what appear to have been the fourth and fifth instalments, although designated the fifth instalment in the *Records*, were issued on March 20, 1789, when the elder Penn received £7,500 and the younger Penn received £22,500. The sixth instalment, which amounted to £25,812 10*s*, was ordered paid a year later. Thus, by the spring of 1790, the Penns were in possession of £100,000 out of the compensation granted them by the State. On April 9, 1791, the Legislature made provision for the appropriation of a sufficient amount of six percent stock created by the State's subscription to a United States loan to discharge the last two instalments, and empowered the governor—the Executive Council had been supplanted by a single executive—to draw the warrants on the State treasurer for all arrearages of principal and interest, whenever the Penns or their agents should apply for the payment of the debt still due them.[9]

---

[8] *Laws of Pa.*, II, 230-234; Scharf and Westcott, *Hist. of Phila.*, I, 406, 407.

[9] *Laws of Pa.*, III, 200; *Statutes at Large of Pa.*, XII, 431-435; XIV, 81-85.

The claim made by the proprietaries on the British government for the losses and sufferings sustained by them in consequence of the Revolution amounted to £944,817 sterling. This was reduced after prolonged investigation by the Commissioners on Loyalists' Claims to £500,000, and that estimate was recommended to Parliament for settlement. On the suggestion of Mr. Pitt, however, that body departed in this instance from its practice of granting a stipulated sum as in the claims of other adherents of the Crown: it passed an act in 1790 by which an annuity of £3,000 was granted to John Penn, the son of the elder branch, and an annuity of £1,000 to John Penn, the son of the younger branch of the family. Sabine remarks that "the Penn estate was by far the largest that was forfeited in America, and perhaps that was ever sequestered during any civil war in either hemisphere"; but he also calls attention to the fact that the large sum which they received from Pennsylvania, together with their annuities from Parliament, the immense estate which they retained in the Commonwealth founded by their ancestor, and the offices subsequently conferred on them probably placed them "in a condition quite as independent as that which they enjoyed previous to the Revolution." Certain it is that the Penns remained the largest landed proprietors in Pennsylvania, by reason of their manors and other real estate, together with the ground rents and quit rents which they derived therefrom.[10]

---

[10] Sabine, *Loyalists of the Am. Rev.*, II, 162, 163; *Colon. Records of Pa.*, XVI, 4, 33, 300, 306; Scharf and Westcott, *Hist. of Phila.*, I, 407.

CHAPTER VI

THE PURCHASE OF THE INDIAN TRACT ON LAKE ERIE

Besides the public domain which the revolutionary government of Pennsylvania took from the proprietaries and the numerous private estates which it confiscated from the attainted Loyalists, a large triangular tract of territory fronting on Lake Erie was acquired from the Six Nation Indians by purchase, notwithstanding the fact that they had allied themselves with the British early in the war, had made Fort Niagara their headquarters, and had engaged in many expeditions with Butler's Rangers against the frontier settlements. The first definite action looking to the purchase of the tract in question was taken by the Assembly, September 25, 1783, when a resolution was adopted by that body authorizing the appointment of purchasing commissioners. These commissioners seem not to have been named by the Executive Council until late in February, 1784, and on December 4th the Council was able to report that the purchase had lately been made. The lands thus secured were offered for sale to white settlers at a price which proved to be too high to attract many buyers; and the Council suggested to the Assembly in a message of February 23, 1787, that the price be lowered, since only eight warrants had been issued for lots within the purchased tract during the past six months.[1]

On September 4, 1788, Congress passed an act by which the United States government relinquished and transferred to the State of Pennsylvania its right, title, and claim to the tract on Lake Erie. As a meeting of the Northern and Western tribes was soon to be held at Muskingum to make a treaty with the Continental commissioners, the State Assembly took action on September 13th, empowering the Council to appoint two commissioners to secure from the forthcoming council a conveyance of its rights in the purchased tract, as the Western tribes had acknowledged claims therein. Accordingly, General Richard Butler and General John Gibson were named as the agents of the Commonwealth to attend the approaching council. The instructions, which were framed for their guid-

---

[1] *Colon. Records of Pa.*, XIV, 45, 271, 273; XV, 167.

ınce, informed the new commissioners that the State was already 'vested with both right of jurisdiction and soil," but that the pur-
:hase of the claims of the natives, which they were to effect, was ıgreeable "to the constant usage of Pennsylvania," and that they vere to exercise their discretion whether to commence the busi-
ıess with the Indians at present, or postpone it until a more fa-
'orable time, according to the temper in which they might find the ribes. Evidently the Indians manifested a friendly disposition, cr on March 4, 1789, the Council sent to the Legislature the report ıf the commissioners that the transaction had been satisfactorily ompleted, together with an Indian deed of cession covering the ract.[2]

---

[2] *Colon. Records of Pa.,* XV, 531, 609; XVI, 36, 37, 139.

CHAPTER VII

THE SURVIVAL OF LOYALISM IN PHILADELPHIA AND ELSEWHERE IN PENNSYLVANIA AFTER THE DEPARTURE OF THE BRITISH

On the day of the evacuation of Philadelphia, June 18, 1778, Captain Allen McLane and his Maryland troopers followed the British as they retreated into the Neck and captured Captain Thomas Sandford of the Bucks County Light Dragoons and Frederick Varnum, keeper of the prison under Galloway. On the next day the American forces re-entered Philadelphia, and Major General Benedict Arnold was made commandant of the city. Arnold at once issued a proclamation calling attention to the resolution of Congress of June 4th, which requested Washington to see that order was preserved in the town and to prevent the removal or sale of the King's goods that remained in the possession of the people. Persons having a supply of certain articles, including all kinds of provisions beyond family need, were to make return to the town major. A large quantity of salt and other supplies were discovered and seized under this order. Severe punishment was to be meted out to any found concealing British officers or soldiers or deserters from the Continental army. On June 20th, the city and its markets were declared open, and on the 25th and 26th, Congress and the Supreme Executive Council, respectively, began their sessions in the city.

The returning inhabitants had many complaints to make concerning the damage or removal of their property by the departing host, one giving notice that "Joseph Fox, a noted traitor, had seized and taken away four tons of blistered steel, and all the apparatus belonging to the steel furnace," which he had sold in the city; while another reported the removal of a printing press and its belongings, which were carted away in the King's wagons by James Robertson, the Tory printer of the *Pennsylvania Gazette*. In August, Arnold had a court-martial held for the trial of George Spangler and Frederick Verner on the charge of being spies in the British employ. The former was hanged the same month; but the latter was kept in prison until he was finally exchanged. As many other Loyalists remained in Philadelphia, the Whigs preferred charges before Chief Justice Thomas McKean against some of these for aiding the British army, formed an association, afterwards called "the Patriotic Society," with the object of "disclosing and bringing to justice all Tories within their knowledge," and committed an attack on the house of Peter Deshong, who escaped injury by surrendering to the authorities as a proclaimed traitor. In September Deshong, together with several others accused of treason, was tried and acquitted; but Abraham Carlisle of Philadelphia and John Roberts of Lower Marion, two Quakers well along in years, were convicted and, despite the appeals of some members of their juries and of numerous Whigs for commutation of sentence, were executed. Many other prosecutions followed during the months of November and December.[1]

Meanwhile, General Arnold was occupying the mansion of Richard Penn, living in great extravagance, associating chiefly with Tory families, and getting into trouble through his gross venality. Already in December, 1778, it was being rumored among his acquaintances that Arnold would be discharged from his post, "being thought a pert Tory," and soon after that he was behaving "with lenity" towards this class of Philadelphians. In the latter part of March the commandant bought a handsome country estate at Mount Pleasant, which a purchasing agent of General Washington says he paid for by appropriating to his own use $50,000 which the agent left to his order for the liquidation of bills for army stores and clothing. At length, Arnold's corruption and display became so scandalous that the Supreme Executive Council formulated a series of charges against him, which he evaded by leaving the city. By direction of Congress a court-martial was held to try Arnold, but not until in January, 1780. Being convicted on the minor charge of making private use of the army wagons, he was sentenced to receive a reprimand from the commander in chief. He was exasperated by this verdict, and in the following spring he began his traitorous correspondence with General Clinton. In mid-summer he was appointed commander of the fortress of West Point, "the gateway of the Hudson Valley," at his own request by Washington. The arrangements for the surrender of this important post to the British were completed at

---

[1] Scharf and Westcott, *Hist. of Phila.*, I, 885, 886, 887, 894.

Arnold's secret conference with Major John André at Stony Point on a dark night in September; but André was captured immediately afterward near Tarrytown. A letter unsuspectingly sent by Colonel Jameson informed Arnold of the British officer's arrest, and he fled on horseback to the river, where he boarded the enemy's sloop of war *Vulture* under a flag of truce. By October 8th, he was at the head of the American Legion, a corps of Loyalists newly organized by him in New York, which then numbered only 75 troopers. This was the command he got as part of the price of his perfidy; but he also received £6,000 sterling. On October 2d, Arnold's estate at Mount Pleasant was confiscated by the Supreme Executive Council. It was subsequently sold to pay off a mortgage. On October 27th, the Council ordered his Loyalist bride, who was a daughter of Chief Justice Edward Shippen of Philadelphia, to leave the State within two weeks.[2]

A widespread fear of Toryism continued to prevail in Philadelphia after the re-occupation of the city by the Americans. During 1779 a number of supposed British sympathizers were prosecuted on various charges; but most of them were acquitted, and a few were discharged because witnesses failed to appear against them, although they were required to give security for their good behavior. Of the few convicted, Samuel R. Fisher, a Quaker, was sentenced to jail for having sent information to the enemy at New York; George Hardy, who was to suffer capital punishment for having helped to disarm citizens of Southwark, was reprieved with the rope around his neck until after the session of the next Assembly; Joseph Pritchard was found guilty of misprision of treason and laid under the penalty of losing his property and being imprisoned during the war, and William Cassedy, *alias* Thompson, was sentenced to death for high treason.[3]

That the community was not disposed to relax its vigilance in regard to the Loyalists is shown also by certain events occurring in the spring of this year. Thus, at the end of March, the Assembly passed a law empowering the officers of the militia to disarm nonjurors within their respective districts against whom sworn information should be given before a justice, permission being granted to the officers to remove cannon and all other warlike

---

[2] Scharf and Westcott, *Hist. of Phila.*, I, 389-393; Rev. W. O. Raymond's Ms. Notes on Col. Edward Winslow's Muster Rolls.

[3] Scharf and Westcott, *Hist. of Phila.*, I, 400.

weapons from buildings belonging to the suspects. In May a public meeting was held to take measures for ascertaining whether inimical persons still remained in the city. Its action resulted in the appointment of a committee to hear evidence against any who might be accused of unfriendliness to the United States. As the proceedings of this committee did not meet with popular approval, the companies of militia formed a committee of their own, which on October 4th arrested several citizens and took them to a tavern on the common, where 200 of the militia also assembled. This body then marched to the house of James Wilson, Esq., a lawyer who had defended certain Tories accused of treason, taking with them two cannon and a number of Quakers and Tories whom they had arrested. Anticipating an attack, Mr. Wilson and his friends were prepared to resist. Before the mob in the street was finally dispersed, an affray occurred in which some persons were injured and three were killed. Twenty-seven of the attacking militiamen were seized and incarcerated, but were admitted to bail the next day. On October 6th the Supreme Executive Council issued a proclamation calling on the other rioters and the inmates of Wilson's house to surrender themselves, pending a judicial inquiry, and some of the latter did so. The Council attributed this tumult to the "undue countenance and encouragement" shown to disaffected persons by "men of rank and character in other respects," as also to the frequent disregard of the laws and public authority of the State. Those who gave themselves up in obedience to the Council's proclamation were bound over in large sums for their appearance at the next session of the Court of Oyer and Terminer. David Solebury Franks, the commissary of British prisoners, who was involved in this affair and had surrendered himself along with the others, was ordered to depart the State but delayed until November 22d, when Joseph Reed, the president of the Council, informed him that he was expected to set out on his journey the next day without further indulgence. As for the others involved in this affair, neither the militia nor Wilson's friends were prosecuted, the Assembly passing an act of amnesty in their behalf on March 13, 1780.[4]

Meanwhile, on August 11, 1779, the Supreme Executive Council asked the chief justice of the State for his opinion regarding

---

[4] *Statutes at Large of Pa.*, IX, 346-348; *Colon. Records of Pa.*, XII, 121, 130, 137-139, 145, 152; Scharf and Westcott, *Hist. of Phila.*, I, 401-403; Sabine, *Loyalists of the Am. Rev.*, II, 444, 445; *Laws of Pa.*, II, 257.

the status of certain Pennsylvania Loyalists, who had been captured at sea while engaged in a privateering enterprise and were
already confined in the State prison. The chief justice replied that
such of the prisoners as had not owed allegiance since February
11, 1777 (when the law defining treason and misprision of treason
was enacted by the Assembly), were to be deemed prisoners of war,
while any others might be proceeded against as traitors under the
act of September 8, 1778, establishing a Court of Admiralty. On
September 14, 1779, the Council directed the chief justice to obtain the facts in regard to the prisoners in question and submit
them, together with his advice. What that official reported does
not appear; but it was of such a tenor that the Council ordered the
commissary of prisoners not to exchange his privateering charges
without the further order of the board. On October 1st the Assembly passed a further supplement to the test laws because, as the
supplement stated, many persons had omitted to subscribe to them
probably "from disaffection to our late glorious revolution." In
order, however, to afford all an opportunity to subscribe, the time
for taking the test was extended to December 1st for the inhabitants of Cumberland, Bedford, Northumberland, and Westmoreland counties, thirty-five days being allowed for the inhabitants of
Lancaster, York, Berks, and Northampton counties, and twenty-
days only for the non-jurors of the City and County of Philadelphia, as also for those of Bucks and Chester counties. Persons
refusing to take advantage of these arrangements were declared to
be forever incapable of electing or being elected to office, serving
on juries, or keeping schools, and to be forever deprived of the
privileges and benefits of citizenship. This measure was followed
within a few days by one authorizing the Council and the justices
of the Supreme Court to order the arrest of suspects and to increase the fines of persons neglecting their militia duty.[5]

The enactment of such laws indicate that the authorities still
had many Loyalists to deal with. The popular resentment against
this class of inhabitants had vented itself upon the male sex; and
with but few exceptions the action of the Supreme Executive Council and the other bodies that were entrusted with the promotion
of the cause of liberty had been diected against members of the
same sex. But in June, 1779, the grand jury had made a present-

---

[5] *Colon. Records of Pa.*, XII, 71, 74, 103, 112; *Statutes at Large of Pa.*, IX, 277-283, 404-
407; *Laws of Pa.*, II, 219.

ment to the effect that the wives of British emissaries had not departed and were keeping up an injurious correspondence with the
enemies of the country, supplying them with intelligence and
propagating the most poisonous falsehoods. This action appears
to have produced no marked effect in causing the wives of absent
Loyalists to follow their husbands into exile, so far as official records show.   During the entire year of 1779 the Council issued
scarcely more than a score of passports to such persons. One of
these was granted to Mrs. Jacob Duché and her children; but on
July 1st another pass was issued to the same family to return on
account of Mrs. Duché's ill-health. Under date of February 4, 1780,
an entry appears in the minutes of the Council that Elizabeth
Fegan, the wife of an attainted traitor, was still lingering in Philadelphia, after having been accorded permission to go to New York,
and that if she should be found within the State ten days from
date, she was to be arrested and confined in the common jail. The
record shows that a few passes in the usual form, that is, on condition that the applicant should not return or must obtain the
Council's consent before doing so, were granted during this month.
It was not until March 7th of this year that the Council reached the
conclusion that the grand jury had reached nine months before,
being constrained thereto no doubt by the discovery in an intercepted journal that Mrs. Samuel Shoemaker, whose husband was
with the enemy, had been assisting prisoners and other persons
inimical to the American cause to pass secretly to New York. At
the same time the power to pardon persons under sentence of death
for treason was vested by legislative act in the Executive Council,
on condition that such persons would depart to foreign lands and
not return to the United States. The Council now decided to publish notice that passports would be granted before April 15th to
Loyalist wives to go within the British lines to their respective
husbands, and that their neglect of proceeding thither would render it necessary to take further measures for the purpose. Only
two women seem to have responded to this action, one of these being Mrs. Shoemaker, who did not secure her pass until April 16th,
and had the courage to ask to be allowed to return within a year,
but was subjected to the condition of obtaining the Council's consent. On June 6th the Council announced that public notice would
be given to the wives and children of such persons as had joined the
enemy, requiring their departure from the State within ten days,

and that protection would then be withdrawn from any remaining, who would become liable to prosecution as enemies of the State. A second clause of this order added that anyone carrying letters to or from New York or other places in the possession of the British would be subject to legal action, unless the letters had been inspected and properly endorsed by a member of the Council, or of the Continental Board of War, or by the commissary of prisoners; and it was recommended that offenders be taken before a justice of the peace for commitment until the further order of the Council. On June 13th passports were issued to seven women under the terms of the new order, and on June 16th to ten more. The ten days specified in the resolution had now elapsed; but during the next thirty days the Council had to enforce its decree by directing that several wives, who had failed to depart, should be put in the workhouse, until they should give security to leave the State and not return again. During October several more women were sent to join their husbands, including Mrs. Esther Yeldall, the wife of Dr. Anthony Yeldall, who was required to take her five children with her and furnish bond in the sum of $20,000 not to return to any of the States during the war. Permission was granted during the same month to William Hamilton to sail for St. Eustatia and to Thomas Mendenhall to proceed to Ireland by way of New York. On December 18th Joseph Stansbury and his family were offered the privilege of going within the British lines. Mr. Stansbury had been included in the proclamation of attainder published on June 15, 1778. In 1780 he was arrested and imprisoned in Philadelphia on the charge of engaging in illicit trade with the enemy, but in December was allowed to remove with his family and effects to New York, on condition that he would "use his utmost endeavors" to have two American prisoners on Long Island returned. On December 21st his request for his books and papers was granted by the Supreme Executive Council; and on the 8th of the following month a passport was issued to Mrs. Stansbury, her six children, and her maid servant. We hear nothing more of this exiled family until February 21, 1781, when they were together in New York City and were put in the way of drawing rations from the British commissary department. From May 1 to the end of June, 1782, Mr. Stansbury was employed in the secret service. In June of the following year he retired with his family to Moorestown, N. J., where he had hired a house, but was at once arrested under a war-

rant from Governor Livingston and ordered to return to New
York. Here on August 9th he was supplied with a letter of recommendation from General Sir Guy Carleton to Governor John Parr,
inasmuch as he was about to sail with his household for Nova
Scotia.[6]

During 1781 a few passports were granted to women to go to
New York, on condition of not returning during the war, and one
on the same condition to Margaret Maguire, whose destination was
Charlestown (S. C.?). But with the advent of the next year a
marked change in the character of the passports is to be noted.
Although numbers of passports continued to be issued during the
remainder of the war, a large proportion of them name other des-
tinations than New York, and even those which name that metropolis provide for the return of the applicant. This is not in-
variably true, for several exceptions occur during the fall, winter,
and spring of 1782-83; and a group of four within this period des-
ignate Newburyport, while denying the right to return. In February, 1783, one applicant is permitted and another refused the
privilege of going to Nova Scotia; and on April 17th the Honorable
John Penn, his wife, and attendants are authorized to proceed to
New York. If the Council's formula "not to return" or "not to return during the war" be taken as a criterion of the Royalist at-
tachments of those to whom it was applied, over ninety such were
supplied with passports during the period of eighteen months from
the beginning of September, 1778, to the end of July, 1783. Of
these ninety or more, thirteen were men; the others were women
with a few children. In most cases the destination was New York;
but four passports were issued for Newburyport; two for Halifax,
one for Nova Scotia, one for Charlestown, one for St. Eustatia, one
for Ireland, one for Germany, and two for Europe.

Not only the wives of Loyalists who had joined the enemy
proved particularly troublesome during the early months of 1780;
but the Quakers also, both in the City and County of Philadelphia,
proved to be a disturbing element by declining to furnish information in regard to the amount of their property for the purposes of
taxation, although such concealment rendered them liable to a four-
fold assessment. Then, too, the resident Loyalists were so active

[6] *Colon. Records of Pa.*, XI, 43, 518, 571, 642, 649, 673, 758; XII, 11, 21, 24, 29, 36, 44,
61, 68, 69, 79, 81, 101, 120, 243, 253, 256, 257, 270, 271, 300, 352, 377, *passim;* XIII, 17, 21,
30, 59, *passim; Rep. on Am. Mss. in the Roy. Inst. of Gt. Brit.*, II, 248; III, 85; IV, 216, 269;
Laws of Pa., II, 253, 254.

in intrigues of various kinds that the principal Continental officers in Philadelphia, headed by General Anthony Wayne, published an address on April 6th declaring their "fixed and unalterable resolution to curb the spirit of insolence and audacity, manifested by the deluded and disaffected" by refusing to associate or communicate with anyone who had exhibited "an inimical disposition, or even lukewarmness to the independence of America," or with anyone who might give countenance to such persons, "however respectable his character or dignified his office." They said further that they would regard any military officers who should contravene the object of their declaration as a proper subject for contempt. Among those who were manifesting their inimical disposition at this time were several persons taken up for aiding British prisoners and other enemies of the State to escape. One of those arrested was Dr. William Cooper of Philadelphia, who had concealed a Loyalist for some time and had then procured him a doctor's place on board an armed ship. As Dr. Cooper chose to depart rather than give security for his good behavior in the future, he was granted two months in which to prepare. John Kugler, his wife Susanna, and Abraham Harvey, who were examined by the Council on the charge of helping prisoners and others to flee to New York, Mrs. Kugler being also charged with harboring spies, were sentenced to jail. The same punishment was visited upon James Scott and Henry Lane, two former inhabitants of Philadelphia, who had recently returned to the city.[7]

With so much active Toryism abroad at a time when the outlook for the American cause was peculiarly discouraging, the Supreme Executive Council decided on June 6th in favor of discriminating between the friends of independence and the non-jurors in exacting supplies to meet the pressing needs of the army. Three days later the Council proclaimed martial law in Philadelphia and announced the establishment of an Office of Enquiry to be conducted by commissioners for the arrest of all suspicious characters and to take such other measures as the public safety might require, on the ground that the admission of strangers into the city without examination was enabling the enemy to send in spies and emissaries, distribute counterfeit money, and employ other means to defeat the public welfare. All civil and military of-

---

[7] Scharf and Westcott, *Hist. of Phila.*, I, 408, 410; *Colon. Records of Pa.*, XII, 272, 301, 307, 380, 339, 342.

ficers and other faithful inhabitants of the Commonwealth were therefore required to assist the Board of Enquiry in its operations. Horses belonging to Quakers and Loyalists were seized for the use of the army; the houses of persons suspected of disloyalty to America were searched for arms and, in order to facilitate the collection of provisions, an embargo was laid on all outward-bound vessels, except those in the service of France. The immediate occasion of these rigorous measures is to be found in a sudden invasion of New Jersey by the British.[8]

A committee of Friends presented a memorial to the Assembly of 1780, complaining of laws detrimental to their liberties and privileges and explaining that they were restrained by divine ordinances from complying with "tests and declarations to either party" engaged in actual war. The memorial also stated that members of the society had suffered abuse and that some of them had been subjected to oppression by public officials, especially in the enforcement of the militia law. The committee of the Assembly, to which this communication was referred, formulated a series of questions designed to call forth from the Quakers an expression of their sentiments towards the State, and received a reply thereto which the committee characterized as "an evasion of the questions proposed." As the Assembly paid no further attention to the matter, the Quakers soon adopted an address in vindication of their political course.[9]

The Tories, however, were not treated with such leniency by the Executive Council, which admitted to surety, imprisoned, or sent within the enemy's lines suspicious persons; sentenced several to be hanged who were charged with enlisting in the British service, and was responsible for the execution of David Dawson of Chester on December 25th for visiting Philadelphia while in Howe's possession. Phineas Paxton, an inn-keeper of Bucks County, who was tried on the same date with Dawson (June 27th) for aiding in the escape of British prisoners, was forbidden to keep a tavern any longer, required to furnish a bond of £30,000, or more, and was committed to prison until he should comply with these conditions. The next two cases, which arose nearly a fortnight after Paxton's, gave the Council the opportunity of exercising its power of pardon, newly bestowed by act of the General Assem-

---

[8] *Colon. Records of Pa.*, XII, 272, 301, 307, 330, 339, 342, 383, 384; Scharf and Westcott, *Hist. of Phila.*, I, 410, 411.

[9] Scharf and Westcott, *Hist. of Phila.*, I, 411.

bly, and apparently first employed in behalf of Edward Greswold ("Grizzle") and John Wilson, two youthful deserters from Captain Jacob James's troop of Philadelphia Light Dragoons, who had returned, like others who had enlisted under Howe's proclamation, surrendered themselves, and received sentence of death. Later, however, they were fully restored to their former standing as acceptable citizens of the State.

In November it was discovered that a number of inhabitants of Philadelphia, together with certain persons in New Jersey and New York City, were carrying on trade with refugees in the latter place. Lumber was shipped in vessels sailing from Philadelphia with two sets of clearance papers. On arriving at New York the lumber was sold, and the goods purchased with the proceeds were sent to Shrewsbury, N. J., and then were secretly conveyed to Philadelphia. That such trade had been going on for some time appears from a statement published in the *New Jersey Gazette* of Trenton, under date of January 20, 1779. This statement declared that on January 2d a certain Joseph Castle had been apprehended at Mansfield on his way to the enemy in New York, *via* Shrewsbury, without any passport, and was committed to jail in Burlington; that Castle had a number of letters from Tories in Philadelphia to their friends in New York, some of which showed that a constant correspondence was maintained and traffic carried on between refugees in New York and disaffected persons in New Jersey and Pennsylvania, chiefly by way of Shrewsbury where, as a matter of fact, a considerable number of Tories resided. The statement closed with an admonition to magistrates and others to examine suspicious persons traveling to and from Shrewsbury. Notwithstanding this public warning, the Supreme Executive Council did not apprehend some of the participants in it until late in November, 1780, when eleven of these culprits were given a hearing. A few of them were sent to New Jersey for trial; several more were released on bail, and the others were imprisoned. Among those arrested were Joseph Stansbury, who was allowed to go to New York with his family, as we have already seen; Joshua Bunting of Chesterfield, N. J., who kept the stage-house where the agents of the traders stopped, and James Steelman, John Shaw, and William Black, captains of vessels engaged in the trade. The discovery of this long-continued conspiracy resulted in the forming of a "Whig Association," for the purpose of suppressing all intercourse with Loyalists and suspected persons, and many military officers served on the executive committee of the new organization.[10]

Meantime, considerable damage was being inflicted on the commerce of the city by the operations of Tory privateers in Delaware Bay and River, despite the efforts to prevent it by sending out several pilot boats, a Continental packet, and one of the State galleys.[11]

Notwithstanding the Council's unremitting measures in regard to returned and absent Loyalists, that body found its authority over such persons jeopardized by petitions and resolutions addressed to the Assembly, which it claimed were calculated to rescind its decisions. It therefore sent a message to the House, March 27, 1781, in which it denied any desire on its part to restrict the liberty and liberality of the Assembly in the way of special legislation to annul executive proceedings, but ventured to suggest that such legislation necessarily tended to "lessen the weight of the Council," disturb the harmony of government, and would "eventually injure the real interests of the State." It urged that a better way would be to repeal laws openly and explicitly if they were too severe, or reduce the powers of the Council if they were too extensive; and it concluded by asking for a conference with the House. We can only surmise that the result of this conference was in keeping with the views of the Supreme Executive Council, for its authority does not seem to have been materially lessened.[12]

In November of this year a plot to steal away the secret journals and other papers of Congress was discovered. The execution of this plot, which had been concocted by Benedict Arnold, was undertaken by Lieutenant James Moody of the first battalion, New Jersey Volunteers, one of the most daring Loyalists in the King's service, together with his brother, John Moody, and Lawrence Marr. These men had an accomplice in Addison, an Englishman, who was an assistant to the secretary of Congress. While waiting concealed in a house on the Delaware, Lieutenant Moody accidentally learned that his ally had betrayed the plot; that his associates were already taken, and that a party of soldiers had crossed the river in search of him. Managing to escape up the Delaware

---

[10] *Colon. Records of Pa.*, XII, 401, 419; Scharf and Westcott, *Hist. of Phila.*, I, 412, 413; V. J. *Archives*, 2d Ser., III, 33, 34, 89, 94, 368.

[11] Scharf and Westcott, *Hist. of Phila.*, I, 413.

[12] *Colon. Records of Pa.*, XII, 675.

in a small boat, he succeeded in reaching the British lines after a week's time. His brother was hanged on the Philadelphia common before the end of the month; but Lawrence Marr was respited and afterwards released.[13]

The arrest of the Loyalists engaged in the illicit traffic with New York City, which was effected at about the same time that John Moody was executed, did not suffice to put an end to the intercourse between New York and Philadelphia. That intercourse continued, indeed, during the year 1782, being carried on by means of wagons with false bottoms and sides, in which 800 pounds of goods could be stowed away. Articles for shipment were also placed in kegs, which were then hidden in barrels of cider and thus carried to their destination. By a law passed in September " 'for the more effectual suppression of intercourse and commerce with the enemies of America' British goods were declared contraband and liable to forfeiture, while the importer was punishable with three months' imprisonment."[14]

For some time small groups of Pennsylvania Loyalists had been carrying on predatory warfare in the southeastern part of the State. These bands of "robbers," which were well mounted, committed their depredations with such boldness and success that both the Supreme Executive Council and the Legislature were moved to take action against them. On July 17, 1782, the Council, having received information that Thomas Bulla, Stephen Anderson, and John Jackson, three inhabitants of Chester County who had been attainted, were writing letters to various citizens, threatening to burn their houses and effects, issued a proclamation offering a reward of £50 in specie for the arrest and imprisonment of Bulla and of £20 each for the incarceration of the other two. Some months later Gideon Vernon, another attainted Loyalist, returned to Chester County and was harbored by John Briggs, who was sentenced to pay a fine of £50 and suffer imprisonment for a season. On June 3, 1783, however, the Council decided—on petition from Briggs—to remit his term in jail, on condition that he furnish security for the payment of his fine, in addition to the fees and costs of the prosecution and for his good behavior during the next three years. The names of Vernon and Bulla, together with

[13] *Narrative of James Moody;* Sabine, *Loyalists of the Am. Rev.,* II, 48, 95, 97; *Laws of Pa.,* II, 379; Scharf and Westcott, *Hist. of Phila.,* I, 419.
[14] *Ibid.,* 424.

hose of the notorious Doane brothers of Bucks County and eleven
others, appear in a proclamation of the Council, dated September
3, 1783, which quotes a special act of the Assembly authorizing
heir speedy arrest and punishment as persons who have been
luly attainted with complicity in these crimes. As the act offered
a reward of £300 each for the delivery of the offenders to the sher-
ff of any county in the Commonwealth, and also a reward of £50
or the discovery of any one who had aided or comforted them, or
ad received booty stolen by them with the knowledge that it had
een stolen, the Council ordered all judges, justices, sheriffs, and
onstables to make diligent search for the offenders and their abet-
ors. This order and the liberal rewards offered were efficacious, at
east in so far as the Doanes were concerned; although Israel Doane
ad already been captured and put in jail in the previous February.
A petition, which he addressed to the Council for release, on account
of the destitute condition of his family and his own sufferings, was
dismissed. In September, 1783, Joseph Doane, the father of Israel
and his brothers, was in the Bedford County jail. In October, 1784,
Aaron Doane was under sentence of death at Philadelphia, but
vas pardoned by the Council in the following March. Abraham
and Mahlon, two other brothers who were mentioned in the procla-
nation, paid the full penalty for their depredations: they were
anged in Philadelphia.   Moses Doane was shot and killed by his
aptor after a desperate encounter.   Joseph Doane, Jr., while on
ne of his raids, was severely wounded and taken prisoner, but es-
aped from jail and crossed into New Jersey. There he lived under
n assumed name for nearly a year, without giving up his former
mployment. At length he fled to Canada. Sabine tells us that "sev-
ral years after the peace, he returned to Pennsylvania—'a poor,
degraded, broken-down, old man'—to claim a legacy of about £40,
vhich he was allowed to recover, and to depart."[15]

When the contents of the preliminary treaty of peace became
known at the end of the revolutionary struggle, the more violent
Whigs were much dissatisfied with the provisions according Loyal-
sts the right to go to any part of the United States and remain
here for twelve months, while forbidding their persecution or the
uture confiscation of their property. On May 29, 1783, the militia
athered at the State House and adopted resolutions against per-

---

[15] *Colon. Records of Pa.*, XIII, 333, 590, 687-690 ; Sabine, *Loyalists of the Am. Rev.*, I,
81-383.

mission being granted to Tory refugees to return, or remain among Americans who had been faithful to their country; announcing the militia's determination to use all means at command to prevent them from doing so, and expressing a readiness to join with others in sending instructions to their representatives in the Assembly. The resolutions further declared that persons "harboring or entertaining those enemies of the country ought to feel the highest displeasure of the citizens," and called for a town meeting to decide on the method of instructing representatives and such other measures as might appear necessary, and for the appointment of a committee to carry the purpose of the assemblage into effect.

Accordingly, a general meeting of citizens was held at the State House, June 14th, and resolutions of the same general tenor as those adopted by the earlier meeting were agreed to, but with an added clause pledging those present to use every method "to expel with infamy" those refugees who had presumed, or should in future presume, to return, while authorizing a committee to publish their names in the city papers and see to the execution of the resolutions. The meeting asserted its decided conviction that "the restoration of estates forfeited by law" was "incompatible with the peace, the safety, and the dignity of the commonwealth." After the committee had served peremptory notice on a few returned Loyalists, earnest remonstrances were made against its action, which was criticized as being repugnant to the treaty of peace; but no attention was paid to them by the committee.[16]

In truth, more compassion was shown to attainted Loyalists by the Supreme Executive Council than was manifested to these unfortunate refugees by a committee whose only powers were derived from an unauthorized mass meeting.

[16] Scharf and Westcott, *Hist. of Phila.*, I, 427, 428.

CHAPTER VIII

THE PARDON OF ATTAINTED LOYALISTS BY THE SUPREME EXECUTIVE COUNCIL, 1780-1790

As we have already noted, attainted Loyalists were first pardoned by the Council in July, 1780. The clemency exercised in behalf of Frederick Buzzard, February 13, 1784, was of lesser degree, for he had been convicted in Chester County of nothing worse than aiding British prisoners to escape, and had been fined therefor. A third of the amount imposed having been already paid by Mr. Buzzard or his friends, the Council relented on appeal and remitted the remainder. During the next five years the names of eight attainted persons appear in the minutes of the Council as those of applicants for the mercy and forgiveness of that body. In the case of the first two of these persons the action taken was to suspend the attainder until the next session of the General Assembly. In the case of the next five petitioners, full personal pardon was granted, but this does not appear to have carried with it the restoration of confiscated property in a single instance. In the last case contained in our list leave to withdraw the petition was granted, the Council being averse to considering the applicant's claim for a pardon.

Taking up these cases in their order, we shall consider their special features. The first petition in our series was one signed by various inhabitants of Philadelphia in behalf of Matthias Aspden, a former merchant of the city, who had abandoned a business that brought him a profit of £2,000 annually, gone to New York, and sailed in 1776 for Corunna, Spain, on his way to London. Nine years later Mr. Aspden had returned, and his friends had undertaken to secure a pardon for him, although he is said to have hastened back to England on finding that his life was in peril. The petition in his behalf was first read in Council, November 14, 1785; but it was not acted upon until January 19th of the following year, when Mr. Aspden was reprieved until the next session of the Assembly. In April, 1786, this latter body seems to have granted him a full pardon. However, he did not recover his house, wharf, and warehouses in Philadelphia, which had

been confiscated by the State, April 1, 1781, and which were given
to the university. Despite his pardon, Mr. Aspden did not remain
in America; in 1802 he was in France; in 1804 he was traveling
in Italy; in 1815 he was at New York, and in July, 1817, he left
Philadelphia for England by way of Canada. He died in London,
August 9, 1824, leaving a will which Sabine says gave rise to the
most extraordinary suit ever instituted under the confiscation
acts of the Revolution. It was not finally decided until in 1848,
when his American heirs secured a decree in the United States Cir-
cuit Court that gave them property valued at more than $500,000.
This decree was sustained by the Supreme Court against the appeal of the English claimants.[1]   John Potts who, like Matthias
Aspden, was granted a reprieve until the Assembly should have a
chance to act on his case, was, as we already know, one of Sir William Howe's magistrates of the police at Philadelphia, having
served earlier as a judge of the Court of Common Pleas. After retiring to New York he had been attainted in 1779, and at the peace
he probably went to Nova Scotia as a refugee settler. His application for a pardon was favorably considered by the Council on
May 26, 1786.[2]

Of the group of five Loyalists whose requests were fully accorded, it may be remarked in general that none of them was as
prominent or influential as either of the two who had received at
the hands of the Council only suspension of sentence. Moreover,
the first of the five, Thomas Gordon, put forward the claim that he
was under lawful age at the time of his attainder, and he asked
only that the Council would institute process in the Supreme Court
of the State to determine the validity of its sentence in view of the
fact alleged. Gordon's petition was finally granted, November 26,
1787, after the lapse of seven and a half months from the time of
its presentation.[3]   The second petitioner in this group was Robert
Cunard of Norristown, Montgomery County, who, like hundreds of
his fellow-Pennsylvanians, had joined the British army in 1777.
His application was read and concurred in, June 1, 1789. While
there was nothing unusual about the career of Mr. Cunard, he left
descendants in the persons of his grandsons, the offspring of his
son Abraham, a merchant at Halifax, who later became widely

[1] *Colon. Records of Pa.*, XIV, 34, 578, 625; *Sabine, Loyalists of the Am. Rev.*, I, 186-190.
[2] *Colon. Records of Pa.*, XV, 26; Sabine, *Loyalists of the Am. Rev.*, II, 199.
[3] *Colon. Records of Pa.*, XV, 177, 338.

known as the Brothers Cunard, the founders of the Royal Mail Steamship Line.[4] The third applicant in this group was John Wilson of Bucks County, who submitted reasons in his petition why he should be granted a pardon in so far as respected his person only. On hearing this document read, the Council voted "that the said John Wilson be and he is hereby pardoned."[5] A similar action was taken, February 6, 1790, in favor of the fourth petitioner in our list, namely, Arthur Thomas of Philadelphia, who represented that he had "behaved himself peaceably" since his attainder and that he was desirous of returning to Pennsylvania. The fact that Mr. Thomas was recommended to the mercy of the Council by a number of respectable citizens seems to have carried weight with the board, whose secretary not only mentions the recommendation in the records, but also notes that the resolution granting pardon was adopted unanimously. This petitioner, however, did not remain at Philadelphia permanently. In May, 1786, he was living in Wilmington, Del.[6] The last member of this group was John Rankin, who settled at the conclusion of the war in the Quaker colony at Pennfield, N. B., the lands of which he helped to select, being one of the three agents sent from New York City by an association of Pennsylvania Quakers for the purpose. The vicissitudes which this colony passed through in 1787 and the years just following served to disperse many of the settlers at Pennfield, among them being John Rankin, whose petition must have expressed a deep desire of his heart, when he asked to be restored to the rights of citizenship in Pennsylvania. The Council acceded to his prayer on March 9, 1790.[7]

Thus far the Supreme Executive Council had not failed to give a favorable answer to the petitions for pardon that had been submitted to it by relenting or disappointed Loyalists. Finally, however, came the most surprising petition of all, that of the former arch Tory of Pennsylvania, Joseph Galloway, who, after his retirement to England, had stood forth as the irrepressible champion of American Loyalism in his criticisms of the campaigns in the Middle Colonies, in his elaborate discussion of the provisions relating to the Loyalists in the treaty of peace, in his manifold

[4] Colon. Records of Pa., XVI, 107; Sabine, Loyalists of the Am. Rev., I, 346.
[5] Colon. Records of Pa., XVI, 115.
[6] Colon. Records of Pa., XVI, 273; 2d Rep., Bur. of Archives, Ont., (1904), Pt. I, 613.
[7] Vide post, p. 102; Colon. Records of Pa., XVI, 297.

services as agent for his fellow-sufferers, and in his correspondence with many Loyalists who continued in America. So far as one can judge from the entry in the Council's minutes, Mr. Galloway's petition, which was presented by his attorney, Thomas Clifford, was terse and formal, contenting itself with "stating the attainder of the said Galloway of high treason, and praying that Council would be pleased to grant him a pardon of the said offense." It was read the second time on May 18, 1790, "when on motion of the Vice President [George Ross, Esq.], seconded by Mr. [Richard] Willing, it was *Resolved,* That Mr. Clifford have leave to withdraw the said petition." Technically, then, Mr. Galloway's application was not refused: it was withdrawn, and its author remained in England until the time of his death in 1803.[8]

It was probably sometime after this action that a proposal was offered in Council to bestow a general pardon upon such as still rested under the State's proscription. But by a vote of December 3, 1790, the "further consideration" of this motion was postponed until the 7th of the same month, and when that date arrived the consideration of the motion was again postponed. It is more than possible that the recollection of Mr. Galloway's petition was enough to dampen any generous impulses the Council may have felt towards granting amnesty to the mass of offenders who were as yet unpardoned, and that it still preferred to deal individually with such cases as might arise from time to time.

Notwithstanding the popular resentment against Loyalists returning to or remaining in Philadelphia after the peace, many did nevertheless remain, and some did return, besides those who took the precaution to provide themselves with pardons. Of those who continued to reside in Philadelphia Edward Shippen, LL. D., is a notable instance. As we have already seen, his daughter was expelled from the State as the wife of Benedict Arnold, after the latter's treason. Mr. Shippen, however, was not only permitted to remain, but was elevated to the chief justiceship in 1799. This appointment was held by him until his death in 1806. Another of those who found it possible to see the Revolution through without withdrawing from the city was the quaint teacher of Greek and Latin in the Friends' Academy, Robert Proud. He is described as having

---

[8] *Colon. Records of Pa.,* XVI, 363; *Pa. Mag. of Hist. and Biog.,* Vol. XXVI (Dec. 1902), 438; Sabine, *Loyalists of the Am. Rev.,* I, 454-456.

worn a curled gray wig and a half-cocked hat above a Roman nose
and a "most impending brow;" and his letters to his brother show
him to have possessed "high Tory feelings." He is best remembered
by his *History of Pennsylvania*, a work in two volumes, which was
published in 1797 and 1798. He died in 1813, at the age of eighty-
five years. Christopher Sauer, Jr., the Tory printer of Germantown
who left with the British at the evacuation of Philadelphia, came
back later and died near the city in August, 1784. John Parrock,
who had formerly been a resident of the Quaker City, returned from
New York when the British troops and their thousands of Tory
adherents left there in 1783; and although he bore the stigma of
attainder and his property had been confiscated, he remained until
March, 1786, when he proceeded to Halifax. The fact that Chief
Justice Benjamin Chew was sent into temporary exile for refusing
to sign a parole in 1777 did not prevent his entering the State again
after passing through that disagreeable experience, nor did it prevent his being appointed president of the High Court of Errors and
Appeals in 1790. He continued to serve in this capacity until the
tribunal over which he presided was abolished in 1806, which was
only four years before his death. Governor John Penn, who was Mr.
Chew's associate in exile, was supplied with passports to New York
for Mrs. Penn, himself, and their attendants on April 17, 1783.
Whether they were on their way to England at this time does not
appear, although it is probable that they were. If so, Mr. Penn
returned later; for he died in Bucks County in 1795. The Reverend
Jacob Duché, who spent the years of his banishment in England,
recrossed the ocean in 1790 and appeared in Philadelphia shattered
in health, although he survived until 1798.[9]

During 1784 the General Assembly was more or less occupied
in considering proposals to abolish the "test laws." A petition for
their repeal was presented in March, but was laid on the table by
a vote of thirty-seven to twenty-seven. A resolution introduced in
September stated that numbers of young men, who had arrived at
eighteen years of age since the passage of the laws, had not taken
the oaths of allegiance, and were thus being deprived of their citizenship. It called for a law to remedy this condition of affairs, and
was supported by a petition from non-jurors for admission to
political and civic rights. In the course of the discussion that fol-

---

[9] Sabine, *Loyalists of the Am. Rev.*, II, 612, 202, 626, 163; I, 207, 265; *2d Rep., Bur. of Archives, Ont.* (1904), Pt. I, 669; *Colon. Records of Pa.*, XIII, 561.

lowed a resolution was offered in favor of denying the privilege of holding salaried office to citizens who had voluntarily joined the British army, or been convicted of aiding or abetting the King. This resolution was adopted by a vote of forty-six to four. On September 25th a new proposal came up for passage. This was that the test laws be so amended as to entitle all white male inhabitants who had not subscribed, to take the oath under the act of June 13, 1777, and thus become free citizens, but that no person should be eligible to office until he had also taken the oath prescribed in the act of December 5, 1778. This measure was carried by a vote of twenty-nine yeas to twenty-two nays. Three days later the speaker cast the deciding vote in favor of a motion to take up a bill entitled "A further Supplement to the Test Laws," and nineteen members left the Assembly, which was thus deprived of its quorum. The seceders justified their conduct by declaring in an address to the public that improper methods had been employed to force the bill through and insisting that those who had not participated in the toils and sufferings of the Revolution should not share in its benefits. The speaker of the Assembly and other advocates of the revision of the test acts urged in reply that legislation for the relief of non-jurors was necessary, both in order to enfranchise those who had been too young to subscribe to the test act of 1779 and the older men who had been unoffending neutrals during the war and had paid their full proportion of its expense. They estimated that nearly one-half of the inhabitants of Pennsylvania had been deprived of the rights of citizenship by the law of 1779, and added that there could be no danger of any abuse by extending the law since, under its provisions, no person who had joined the British army or had been convicted of aiding and abetting the King was eligible to office.

This question became one of the issues in the election, which was held in October, and the voters in the City and County of Philadelphia, as probably also in other parts of the State, chose candidates for the Assembly who were opposed to the extension of the rights of citizenship to the non-jurors. In December General Anthony Wayne led in the struggle to amend the test laws, adducing as his chief argument that they were depriving of representation many inhabitants who were, nevertheless, subject to taxation, but his amendment was postponed; and a subsequent motion to instruct a committee to report a bill revising the test laws was lost by a vote of eleven ayes to forty-seven nays. Similar efforts during 1785 also ended in failure, although, according to a local historian, the law of 1779 operated with such severity in certain districts of the State that "the number of free men who were entitled to all privileges of citizenship was not sufficient to administer the local government."[10]

Despite this serious condition of affairs, a new test act was passed, March 4, 1786, because—in the words of the act itself—"many of the inhabitants" had failed to subscribe to one or another of the oaths contained in the earlier acts within the times specified, thereby depriving themselves of the privileges of citizenship, and also because it was thought that not a few of the non-jurors would now be willing to testify to their allegiance, since independence was an established fact. It was therefore enacted that non-jurors might take a new test before a justice of the peace of the district in which they lived. The subscribers had to swear or affirm that they renounced all allegiance to King George III., his heirs and successors, that they would bear true faith to Pennsylvania as a free State, and that they had never voluntarily joined or assisted the King, his generals, fleets or armies, or their adherents. Another section of the law declared that no benefit from its provisions should extend to any person attainted of high treason, nor to any one who had "joined, assisted, or countenanced the savages in their depredations." Obviously, this last clause was aimed at that body of Pennsylvanians who had fled during the war to Fort Niagara and Detroit from the Susquehanna and upper Delaware valleys and from Pittsburgh, respectively, and had thereafter coöperated with the Indians in raids against the frontiers. But the new law, although it was enacted three years after the end of the Revolution, failed likewise to show any leniency to the much larger number of Loyalists who, under the stress of circumstances, including persecutions, had sought safety within the enemy's lines, not to speak of those who had enlisted in the royal service. It should be noted that Robert Morris had sought to mitigate the severity of the law by offering two motions, one to strike out certain words describing the new oath as one of "abjuration," and the other to omit the clause in regard to aid rendered to the King, or his generals, fleets, and armies; but both of these motions were lost. The law, therefore, as passed, left no loophole by which unrelenting Loyalists,

[10] Scharf and Westcott, *Hist. of Phila.*, I, 435-436, 439, 440.

whether still within the State or desiring to return to it, might become citizens.[11]

The test law of March 4, 1786, remained in force a little over a year, when it was at length amended, March 29, 1787, about in conformity with the ideas of Robert Morris by the substitution of an oath that was doubtless far less objectionable to the Loyalists. The explanation offered for this action was that the abjuration of the King was no longer effectual, since he had formally renounced the allegiance of the inhabitants of the United States, that many useful citizens were disqualified by their scruples against taking the test as it stood, and that it was impolitic to deprive the community of their allegiance. Henceforth, therefore, the subscriber would only be required to swear to his allegiance to Pennsylvania as an independent State and to abstain from doing anything injurious to the freedom thereof. Those consenting to subscribe to this simple oath were declared free citizens.[12]

It was not, however, until March 13, 1789, that the Assembly reached the point where it was prepared to annul the entire series of test acts, including even that mentioned in the preceding paragraph. All these laws were now declared to be repealed and all non-jurors to be restored to citizenship.[13]

That the animosities between Whigs and Tories were still capable of revival was shown later in the same year in connection with the opposition arising between factions in two Scotch Presbyterian congregations of Philadelphia over the question whether the Associate Presbytery of Pennsylvania should remain subject to the Synod of Edinburgh. One of these factions besought the Assembly for a law annulling this relationship in so far as it concerned the holding of the local church property. The other or Tory faction was opposed to such a measure. Nevertheless, a law was enacted in September, which canceled the declaration of trust between the local presbytery and the parent synod to the extent of releasing the former from subjection to a foreign jurisdiction. As the opposing faction comprised men of influence in Philadelphia, it had been able to delay the passage of the law for several months; and even after the measure had been enacted by a proportionate vote of three to one, this faction attempted in Novem-

---

[11] *Statutes at Large of Pa.*, XII, 178-181.
[12] *Ibid.*, 473-475.
[13] *Ibid.*, XIII, 222-224.

r to induce the Legislature to repeal the act, although without
ccess. While the question at issue was strictly sectarian in
aracter, its political implications aroused general interest and dis-
ssion in the city.[14]

---

[14] Scharf and Westcott, *Hist. of Phila.*, I, 442.

CHAPTER IX

THE SALE OF FORFEITED ESTATES

Since the close of October, 1777, the estates of those who had gone within the British lines had been subject to confiscation by the commissioners of the various counties appointed for the purpose, and some estates had been seized. A register of these was kept by the secretary of the Supreme Executive Council, who was at length ordered by that body, April 12, 1779, to give notice that the realties of thirty-seven persons who were named and of others not named would be "speedily sold by public auction or vendue." Of those whose names were given, fourteen had been citizens of Philadelphia, including Joseph Galloway, Andrew Allen, William Allen, Jr., Jacob Duché, Samuel Shoemaker, and John Young, gentleman; six had been inhabitants of the County of Philadelphia, including John Potts of Pottsgrove, Christopher Sauer, a printer of Germantown, and Henry Hugh Ferguson, Esq., of Graeme Park, late commissary of prisoners for General Howe; three of Bucks and Lancaster counties, respectively; four of Chester County; two of York County; one of Northampton County; two of Trenton, N. J., namely, Peter Campbell, gentleman, and Isaac Allen, attorney at law, and Andrew Elliott, Esq., of New York City.[1]

During August and September, 1779, the Council found it necessary to postpone certain sales until after the next session of the Supreme Court of the State, in order that particular claims or liens upon the properties in question, or certain petitions relating thereto, might be passed upon. The first deed was issued under date of August 5th of the year just named. Early in the following March the Council adopted a resolution that the agents for confiscated estates proceed to the sale of all estates held by attainted persons by less than fee simple title, whether through right of marriage or otherwise, since such estates were proving burdensome to the State. Eight days later (i. e., on March 18th,) the Council appointed a standing committee from among its own members to fix the exact times of sales and of payment previous to the signing

[1] *Ante*, pp. 16, 92; *Colon. Records of Pa.*, XI, 745.

of any deed, because purchasers had been taking advantage of the depreciation of money by neglecting to comply with the conditions of sale, namely, to pay one-fourth of the purchase money in ten days, and the remainder in one month from the time of the sale "to the great injury of the State, and the embarrassment of the sales."[2]

During the nine months since sales of the confiscated estates had begun, they had not been numerous: from August 5 to November 29, 1779, inclusive, there had been but ten sales, three being of properties in Philadelphia, four in the county of the same name, one in the County of Chester, and two in the County of Northampton. Results during the first four months of 1780 were but little better, there being only twelve sales during this interval, namely, two of estates in Philadelphia, seven in the County of Philadelphia, and one each in the counties of Chester, Bucks, and Lancaster. The Council was not satisfied with this showing, especially in the two Philadelphia districts, where it looked as though certain marketable properties were being held back. On May 8, 1780, this dissatisfaction manifested itself in the form of instructions to the agents for the City and County of Philadelphia to proceed to the sale of all forfeited estates within their respective districts, giving due notice thereof according to law. Four days thereafter this order was extended to all the counties, any former order of the Council to the contrary notwithstanding. Sales then continued without official interruption until November 11th, when they were suspended by action of the Council until further notice. However, deeds were again being issued to purchasers at the end of another fortnight. On February 21, 1781, all agents were requested to render a full return of all forfeited estates within their several counties, the names of attainted persons, their real property, the names of purchasers, and the prices at which sales had been made. Eight and a half months later a supplementary report was called for concerning all forfeited estates remaining unsold and the interest held therein, whether in fee simple or otherwise, by the persons who had forfeited them. The only return recorded in the minutes of the Council under this request appears to have been that of Robert Smith, agent for the City of Philadelphia, who reported but three properties in his district. Sales were still in progress as late as December, 1790, up to which time properties of seventy-five per-

[2] *Colon. Records of Pa.*, XII, 73, 76, 77, 80, 82, 103, 273, 281.

sons had been disposed of, and 136 or more deeds had been issued. The names of the attainted owners appearing most frequently in the records of sales listed in the Council's minutes are those of Andrew Allen, Joseph Galloway, Samuel Shoemake, Christopher Sauer, Alexander Bartram, John Parrock, and John Rankin.[3]

A number of the confiscated estates, however, are not listed in the records of sales, for they were appropriated, as we have already seen, to serve as sources of endowment for the University of Pennsylvania. Two properties were similarly appropriated to be used as residences of State officials: thus, the house and lots of Joseph Galloway at the southeast corner of Sixth and Market streets were taken over by act of March 18, 1779, for the benefit of the president of the Supreme Executive Council, while the large mansion of the Reverend Jacob Duché at the northeast corner of Third and Pine streets became the domicile of Chief Justice Mc-Kean. Later the property of Mr. Galloway ceased to be occupied and fell rapidly into a state of decay. By act of April 6, 1786, therefore, the Legislature ordered the Executive Council to advertise it for sale.[4]

In this connection certain cases of confiscation may be mentioned on account of their exceptional character. Proceedings against the estate of Raymond Keen, who presented himself before the chief justice within the time specified and was discharged from prosecution, were declared null and void on his petition to the Assembly. The special act relating to Keen's case restored to him such of his lands and tenements, rights, and credits as had not been sold by the Commissioners for the Sale of Forfeited Estates. The estate of Henry Hugh Ferguson was transferred by legislative authorization of April 2, 1781, to his wife, Elizabeth Ferguson. A preliminary statement is needed to make clear the case of Thomas Gordon. Gordon was a minor in 1778, when he was placed by his mother on board a British vessel in the port of Philadelphia, against his own inclination. As he was still absent from the country on August 5, 1779, by which time he should have presented himself for trial under a proclamation of attainder, his estate was confiscated. Later he returned to Philadelphia and applied to the Assembly for the restoration of his property, and his

---

[3] *Colon. Records of Pa.*, XII, 341, 347, 539, 634; XIII, 106, 141; XIV, 56, 657, 665; XV, 4, 14, 43, 185, 193, 230, 468, 648; XVI, 283, 299, 309, 320, 387, 390, 422.

[4] *Laws of Pa.*, II, 204; 236; Scharf and Westcott, *Hist. of Phila.*, I, 396, n. 8.

petition was granted by act of March 29, 1788. It was afterwards discovered, however, that the commissioners had disposed of his estate; and on September 27, 1791, the Assembly directed the comptroller general to give Gordon a certificate for the money received by the State on account of the sale of his property, including interest at the rate of six percent from the date of sale.[5]

---

[5] *Laws of Pa.*, II, 216, 217, 287; Sabine, *Loyalists of the Am. Rev.*, I, 597; *Statutes at Large of Pa.*, XIII, 67, 68; XIV, 140, 141.

CHAPTER X

THE EMIGRATION OF PENNSYLVANIA LOYALISTS

I. FLIGHTS TO ENGLAND

The first Loyalists so far as known to leave Philadelphia for England were Richard Penn and Judge Samuel Curwen, both of whom took their departure in 1775. The latter remained in the mother country until the end of July, 1784, when he sailed for Boston, Mass., where he arrived on the 25th of the following September. He spent the remainder of his days in his native land. Mr. Penn had been governor of Pennsylvania from 1771 to 1773, and had then served as a member of the Council and as a naval officer of the Colony under his brother, Governor John Penn; but on returning to England, he was entrusted with the second petition of Congress to the King. He died in Britain in 1811. It was reported that the Reverend Jacob Duché sailed from Philadelphia in December, 1777. As he had acted for three months as chaplain to the first Continental Congress, he seems to have felt the need of conciliating his ecclesiastical superiors in England. In the spring of 1780 he was followed across the water by his wife and children, who sailed from New York. Mr. Duché returned to Philadelphia in 1790, after an exile of twelve years. He died eight years later. The fugitive governor of New Hampshire, John Wentworth, stopped at the Quaker City early in 1778 on his way to London, where he arrived—according to Governor Hutchinson's *Diary*—on March 13th, after a passage of twenty-four days. A week later Mr. Hutchinson records that he received a call from his fellow-exile who, we may add, had been granted an annual allowance of £500 twelve months before by the Lords of the Treasury. When General Howe left Philadelphia on his homeward voyage about the middle of May, 1778, it was stated in one of the newspapers that he was accompanied by some of the refugees. This was probably true. At any rate, there were a few Pennsylvanians in London in July, 1779, at which time they signed an address to the King. Among them were Thomas Bank, Peter Biggs, Charles Eddy of Philadelphia, Jabez Maud Fisher, William Harris, and John Johnson. Joseph

Galloway sailed from New York for England with his only daughter in October, 1778, from which time he was paid, like Governor Wentworth, £500 per annum from the Treasury.[1] In London he told Governor Hutchinson, whose acquaintance he made early in the following December, that all Pennsylvania and New Jersey would have returned to their allegiance if the British army had not moved from Philadelphia, that they would still do so under a proper prosecution of the war, the past conduct of which he sweepingly condemned, and he expressed the opinion that the Middle Colonies were tired of the contest. On another occasion he mentioned to Hutchinson his having applied to General Howe, as soon as he had heard that Philadelphia was to be evacuated, to learn what was to become of the magistrates of the city, and said that Howe had advised them to make terms with General Washington under a flag of truce, but that Clinton had assured them that America would be vanquished and that their salaries should be continued to them. Galloway sought to convince the British authorities that less than one-fifth of his fellow-countrymen favored the Revolution, which had been strengthened by disarming and intimidating the Loyalists, that under adequate protection and assistance most of the people would openly support the royal government, and that more efficient measures would soon reduce America. In June, 1779, the House of Commons instituted an investigation into the American war, Mr. Galloway serving as one of the most important witnesses. His testimony was so damaging and dealt so severely with the operations of the commanding officers in America that the investigation was dropped. But Mr. Galloway continued the agitation through pamphlets and letters, the object of which was to convince the English people and government that the subjugation of America was not only feasible, but was also necessary for the maintenance of the British power in the world. When peace was made, another pamphlet was published by the distinguished refugee from Philadelphia, in which he examined unsparingly that clause in the treaty which related to the Loyalists. As agent for this class of war sufferers, he rendered valuable service, his daughter declaring that "for twenty years his morning room was often

---

[1] Curwen's *Journal and Letters*, 414, 415; Sabine, *Loyalists of the Am. Rev.*, II, 164; I, 390; *Pa. Mag. of Hist. and Biog.*, II, 68-73; *Diary and Letters of Thos. Hutchinson*, II, 192, 194; *Rep. on Am. Mss. in the Roy. Inst. of Gt. Brit.*, I, 94; *N. J. Arch.*, 2d Ser., II, 220; Sabine, *Loyalists* II, 164, 350, 388; I, 454; *2d Rep. Bur. of Arch., Ont.*, (1904), II, 1169

crowded, and seldom empty of Americans who received from him his best services in their own affairs." Mr. Galloway died at Watford, Herts, England, August 29, 1803, in his seventy-first year.[2]

It would be interesting to know something of the arrival of the several thousands of refugees from Philadelphia at New York, and what public provision was made for them in a city to which large numbers of such people had been resorting since the summer of 1776, when the British took possession of Staten and Long islands and of the neighboring metropolis. That special accommodations were necessary appears from the statement of David Mathews, the mayor of New York, who reported, August 25, 1783, that after the evacuation of Philadelphia and the second great fire in New York he was directed by General Clinton to proceed according to earlier orders for the purpose of providing for the distressed refugeees, namely, "to grant, without fee or reward, permission to erect temporary habitations on the vacant lots of persons residing without the lines," Mr. Mathews adding that "the lots were held by the erectors of the tenements only during pleasure."[3]

Among those Pennsylvanians who, like Galloway, withdrew to England from New York were some who, together with many of their fellow-countrymen from other States, waited until the evacuation of the metropolis was near at hand before doing so. A few among these were, on petition to the Treasury Board in London, granted financial support in substantial amounts. Thus, Samuel Shoemaker, Daniel Coxe, and John Potts, the former magistrates of police at Philadelphia, were given £200 a year each a little more than a year after their arrival in New York; and Arodi Thayer, who had been tide surveyor at Philadelphia, had his salary continued at the rate of £80 per annum. Inasmuch as the commander in chief was constantly being petitioned by Loyalist families in the city for relief in one form or another, especially from the spring of 1779 on to the fall of 1783, he constituted a committee or board consisting of Mr. Shoemaker, Colonel Beverley Robinson of New Jersey, and Robert Alexander of Maryland; and on October 2, 1782, he ordered "that all memorials cognizable by the Board which assembles at Mr. Shoemaker's may be sent there and proceeded on without a reference from Head Quarters." It was added that the

[2] *Diary and Letters of Thomas Hutchinson,* II, 226, 259; *Pa. Mag. of Hist. and Biog.,* XXVI, 438, 439.

[3] *Rep. on Am. Mss. in the Roy. Inst. of Gt. Brit.,* IV, 308.

people were to be sent there with their memorials. At the end of this year the quarterly allowances from September 30th which the Board recommended for various refugees totaled £1,075, or £1,410 New York currency. Not only did Mr. Shoemaker serve as a member of this board of relief, but he also interceded with the British admiral in behalf of Whig prisoners and was successful in having numbers of them liberated and sent home. At length, in August, 1783, he sailed for England with his son Edward. Before doing so, however, he sent word to the vice-president of the Council of Pennsylvania, that he would cheerfully surrender the papers relating to Philadelphia that were in his possession to any person authorized to receive them. While in London he was often consulted by the Commissioners appointed to settle the claims advanced by Loyalists for the losses they had suffered.[4] If memorials and letters of recommendation from the commander in chief, Sir Guy Carleton, are an indication, not a few Pennsylvanians were preparing to follow Mr. Shoemaker to London in the autumn of 1783. Among these persons were Messrs. Potts and Coxe, who received letters of recommendation to Lord North bearing the date of November 13th. Another Tory who had been prominent in the life of Philadelphia, and who crossed the Atlantic after the peace, was James Humphreys, Jr., the former publisher of the *Pennsylvania Ledger*. However, he soon proceeded to Shelburne, N. S., but returned to Philadelphia in 1797, where he engaged in the printing and book publishing business until his death in February, 1810. His fellow-townsman, Isaac Hunt, who, after being carted through the streets of the Quaker City by a mob, fled to the West Indies and took church orders there, removed later to England and became a tutor in the family of the Duke of Chandos. Mr. Hunt was the brother-in-law of the artist, Benjamin West, and the father of James Henry Leigh Hunt, who died in 1859, after winning renown as a poet and miscellaneous writer. The distinguished Philadelphia physician, Phineas Bond, who was one of the founders of the University of Pennsylvania and a professor in that institution, also appears to have retired to the mother country for a few years; but in 1786 he was appointed British consul for the Middle States. After some hesitation on the part of Congress,

---

[4] *Rep. on Am. Mss. in the Roy. Inst. of Gt. Brit.*, II, 7; III, 125, 169, 136, 148, 221, 294, 422; Sabine, *Loyalists of the Am. Rev.*, II, 301.

he was received in his official capacity and continued as consul for many years.[5]

II. THE MIGRATION TO NOVA SCOTIA

Aside from this notable group of Pennsylvanians and temporary residents at Philadelphia who went to England, and for the most part remained there, a considerable number settled in Nova Scotia. Of these, many families found homes in the new Loyalist city of Shelburne. Sabine in his *Loyalists of the American Revolution* gives the names of more than four score men from Pennsylvania, most of whom received town lots there by grant of the government, on which they settled with their families. These grantees included some successful merchants, chiefly from Philadelphia, who had sustained larger or smaller financial losses as the result of the war: as, for example, Alexander Bertram, whose forfeiture was estimated at £5,000; William Briggs, who is said to have suffered to the extent of £3,000; Henry Guest, whose loss was placed at £1,000, and others, who had been injured in lesser amounts. Other men of prominence who took up their abodes at Shelburne were James Allen of Philadelphia, with his family of four persons; John Boyd, a surgeon from the Quaker City, and Benjamin Booth, one of its merchants, who acted as secretary of the loyal refugees in New York City in 1778. Lieutenant Colonel Abraham Van Buskirk with three other officers and a few privates of the 3d battalion of the New Jersey Volunteers settled in Shelburne, after leaving New York for that destination at the end of September, 1783. Colonel Van Buskirk was soon elected mayor of the town.[6] That many of these men remained in affluent circumstances, despite their losses, is indicated by the fact that they did not leave their servants behind in removing to Nova Scotia. Other places, such as Halifax, Annapolis, Digby, Rawdon, Granville, Argyle, and Ship Harbor, appear to have made but slight gains in population from Pennsylvania. Among those who located in Halifax was Dr. James Boggs, who had been a member of the medical staff of the royal army during the Revolution, and was for many years after 1783 surgeon of the forces at the Nova Scotian capital. John Parrock returned from New York to Philadelphia

---

[5] *Rep. on Am. Mss. in the Roy. Inst. of Gt. Brit.*, IV, 454, 435, 436, 446, 470; Sabine, *Loyalists of the Am. Rev.*, I, 554, 555, 535; II, 472, 473, 482-485, 488, *passim*.

[6] *Rep. on Am. Mss. in the Roy. Inst. of Gt. Brit.*, IV, 375, 376; Sabine, *Loyalists of the Am. Rev.*, I, 235; II, 376; II, 482, 483.

at the close of the war, but in March, 1786, sailed for Halifax with the purpose of engaging in the whaling business.[7]

Of the Tory regiments which had been formed in or near Philadelphia parts of two are known to have located in Nova Scotia, namely, the Philadelphia Light Dragoons and the British Legion. The Legion had been organized under General Sir Henry Clinton's orders by Colonels Lord Cathcart and Bannister Tarleton in May and June, 1778; and in the winter of 1781 it appears to have absorbed the Philadelphia Light Dragoons. At the close of April, 1782, the Legion was stationed at New Utrecht near Brooklyn, L. I. It then numbered 471 men, of whom more than two-thirds were cavalry. At the end of September, 1783, about eighty of these men were still at Brooklyn, the rest having embarked earlier in the same month with Major George Hanger for Halifax. Port Mouton in Queen's County, N. S., was allotted to the British Legion, and a number of houses were at once erected there; but on the discovery in the following spring that the soil was barren and stony, the settlers began preparations for removal. They were interrupted, however, by an accidental fire, which destroyed the town and reduced them to the verge of starvation. The authorities at Halifax promptly despatched a vessel laden with provisions, thus averting the threatened famine. Most of the members of this disbanded corps removed at once to Chedabucto Bay at the eastern end of Nova Scotia, where they founded the town of Guysborough.[8]

III. THE MIGRATION TO NEW BRUNSWICK

Although Nova Scotia proper must have received at the evacuation of New York City and the neighboring islands in the fall of 1783 at least 800 former residents of Pennsylvania, the Province of New Brunswick (which was created in 1784) probably gained the larger share of these people; for most, if not all, of the Loyalist regiments which contained Pennsylvanians were disbanded and given crown lands in New Brunswick; and one large association of Pennsylvania Quakers settled together at Pennfield on the north shore of the Bay of Fundy. Sabine, who had the use of the original agreement among the founders of Pennfield, asserts that it was formulated in 1782. Presumably, it was under

[7] Sec. Rep., Bur. of Archives, Ont. (1904), Pt. I, 129, 195, 196, 517, 518, 669, 537, 564, 565, 580.

[8] Rep. on Am. Mss. in the Roy. Inst. of Gt. Brit., IV, 349, 367, 375; Haliburton, Hist. of Nova Scotia, II, 148, 149.

this agreement that a meeting of Quakers was held at the house of Joshua Knight, 36 Chatham Street, New York City, on July 5, 1783, in order to decide some matters of importance in connection with their plans. At this meeting Samuel Fairlamb, John Rankin, and George Brown were appointed agents to locate lands for the association and to transact any business incident to the occupation of these lands. The agents soon submitted a memorial to Sir Guy Carleton asking the privilege of seeking lands for about sixty families on the River St. John, or elsewhere in that region where suitable ungranted lands might be had; and Carleton forwarded this document under date of August 9th to Governor John Parr at Halifax. The site selected was at Beaver Harbor, which lies north of the island of Grand Manan; and by October the new settlement was already in existence. ⁻One hundred and forty-nine lots were included in the original grant. That incoming settlers rapidly joined the colony is shown by the statement of a writer who, shortly after its foundation, estimated the number of its inhabitants at 800. According to an old plan in the British Museum, there were "fifteen streets and 950 lots in the town proper, with large tracts laid out in farm and garden lots beyond." The County of Charlotte, in which Pennfield was situated, was established June 4, 1785; and the Parish of Pennfield was erected in the following year. It was agreed to build a small meeting house, July 7, 1786, on ground allotted for that purpose. We are told that a fire devastated the town in 1787, which must have greatly increased the distress and want among the pioneers at Pennfield. About the time of the fire, however, partial relief was afforded through the efforts of two Quaker gentlemen from Philadelphia who had visited Beaver Harbor a twelvemonth before, and on their return home had raised a subscription with which they bought and shipped 240 barrels of flour and Indian meal, together with some other necessaries, to be distributed among their destitute brethren. Possibly through the instrumentality of the same gentlemen donations were also received from persons in England during the winter of 1788-89. Whatever recovery Pennfield made from its first conflagration was wiped out by a forest fire in 1790, which left but one dwelling house standing. According to a recent writer, "a few of the inhabitants, including the family of Joshua Knight, remained or came back to rebuild their dwellings at or near the old sites"; but some of the settlers removed to Pennfield Ridge, others to

Mace's Bay, and still others went elsewhere. In June, 1803, the population of the Parish of Pennfield, which continued to consist of Quakers principally, numbered only fifty-four. This little community occupied a good tract of land and lived chiefly by farming, although it sustained two saw-mills and had recently launched two vessels of 250 tons burden each.[9]

We may now turn to the settling of the enlisted men from Pennsylvania, together with their families, in New Brunswick. After the cessation of hostilities the City of Philadelphia, which had been the scene of so much recruiting among the Tory residents and refugees during the British occupation, adopted the following resolution: "That the people of this town will at all times, as they have ever done, to the utmost of their power oppose every enemy to the just rights and liberties of mankind: That after so wicked a conspiracy against those rights and liberties by certain ingrates, most of them natives of these States, and who have been refugees and declared traitors to their country, it is the opinion of this town that they ought never to be suffered to return, but be excluded from having lot or portion among us. And the Committee of Correspondence is hereby requested to write to the several towns in this Commonwealth and desire them to come into the same or similar resolves if they shall think fit." The determination by the victorious party to exclude the Loyalists illustrated by the above resolution, although it was not consistently enforced even in Philadelphia, was prevalent throughout most of the States, and was recognized by the officers of the Loyalist regiments at New York.

These officers therefore submitted their case to Sir Guy Carleton in a letter dated March 14, 1783, saying that whatever stipulations might be made at the peace for the restoration of the property of the Loyalists and for their return home, yet, should the American States be severed from the British Empire, it would be impossible for those who had borne the King's arms to remain in the country. They maintained that the personal animosities arising from civil dissensions had been so heightened by the blood shed in the contest that the opposing parties could never be reconciled. They spoke of the personal sacrifices made by the

---

[9] Sabine, *Loyalists of the Am. Rev.*, I, 607; *Coll. N. B. Hist. Soc.*, No. 4, 73–80; *Rep. on Am. Mss. in the Roy. Inst. of Gt. Brit.*, IV, 269, 270; *Winslow Papers*, 490; Vroom, *Courier Series*, LXXII; Ganong, *Monograph of the Origins of the Settlements in N. B.*, 144, 158.

For some of the Pennsylvania Quakers who settled at Pennfield, see Sabine's *Loyalists of the Am. Rev.*, II, 514, 515, 525, 543, 550, 568, 569, 570, 579, 582, 588, 591, 592, 593, 597, 598.

Loyalists; of the anxiety they felt for the future of their wives and children; of the fidelity of the troops; and of the great number of men incapacitated by wounds, many of them with families who had seen better days. They therefore asked for grants of land in some of the royal American provinces and for assistance in forming settlements, in order that they and their children might enjoy the boon of British government. They also requested pensions for such non-commissioned officers and men as had been disabled by wounds and for the widows and orphans of deceased officers and soldiers, besides permanent rank and half-pay for the officers on the reduction of their regiments. This letter was signed by the commanders of fourteen provincial regiments; and its requests were all eventually complied with.[10]

Indeed, steps were taken within a month after the presentation of the letter looking to the location of the lands asked for by the officers, when several of the petitioners were themselves appointed agents to go to Nova Scotia for this purpose. These agents were Lieutenant Colonels Edward Winslow, Isaac Allen, Stephen DeLancey, and Major Thomas Barclay, who spent the spring and summer of 1783 in exploring the River St. John from St. Ann's Point (Fredericton) for about 100 miles upwards, completing their work and returning before the end of July. Winslow then secured authority at Halifax to lay out blocks of land for the several regiments, in keeping with the suggestions of Sir Guy Carleton that the allotments should be by corps and as near to each other as possible, with the officers' lands interspersed among those of the men so that the settlers might be united and ready for defense in case of an attack on the colony. These blocks were afterwards known as "the twelve mile tracts."

In August, 1783, the royal instructions relative to the disposal of the troops at New York arrived; and on September 12th Carleton ordered Lieutenant Colonel Richard Hewlett of the 3d battalion of DeLancey's Brigade to assume command of the principal British American regiments, which had already embarked nine days before at Brooklyn, having been encamped during the summer at Newtown, L. I., Hewlett was to accompany these troops, already considerably depleted through losses and departures with and without formal discharge, to the River St. John, and take the proper measures to get them promptly to the locations

---

[10] Raymond, *The River St. John*, 531-533.

assigned for their settlement. They sailed with a quantity of necessary stores on the 15th, and on the day following, Brigadier General H. E. Fox and his military secretary, Edward Winslow, left for St. John to inspect the lands up the river and arrange for the reception of the regiments. According to the figures of the commissary general's office at New York, about 4,000 persons connected with the Loyalist regiments sailed for the St. John up to October 12th. Not less than 5,000 had embarked for the same destination earlier in the same year, and a small number went after the departure of the regiments, which arrived on September 27th. Three days later they disembarked and encamped above the Falls; and by October 13th they were disbanded for the most part, and were going up the river as fast as the scarcity of small craft on which they had to depend for conveyance would admit. In December the last of the transports from New York arrived, bringing a supply of clothing and provisions, in addition to her passengers, who were chiefly women and children.[11]

Soon after their coming, the regiments drew for their blocks of reserved land, which were shown and numbered on a plan of the river prepared by the surveyor general of Nova Scotia; but as yet lots had not been surveyed for individual settlers. The tracts drawn by several of the regiments were too remote for their liking; the season was already far advanced, and the difficulty of transport was great. Hence, many of the disbanded officers and soldiers preferred to spend the winter at the mouth of the river, and not a few of them drew lots in the Lower Cove district of Parrtown (St. John), which was laid out for the refugees in December, 1783. Both those who remained here and those who pushed on up the river, except a few of the latter who found shelter in the houses of the old inhabitants, were compelled to endure the severities of a bitter season in rude huts or in canvas tents thatched with spruce boughs and banked with snow. Needless to say, the women and children suffered most, and numbers of them did not survive through the winter. Among the Pennsylvanians, who were grantees of Parrtown, were Joseph Canby, John Chubb of Philadelphia, and Ross Currie, a lieutenant of the Pennsylvania Loyalists, who received half pay and became one of the first practitioners of law in the new community; while Robert Stackhouse of Mount Bethel,

---

[11] Siebert, "The Refugee Loyalists of Connecticut" in *Trans. Roy. Soc. of Canada*, 1916, 89, 90; Raymond, *The River St. John*, 536, ff.; *Winslow Papers*, 131-133, 141.

Pa., was a grantee of Carleton, another Loyalist town which sprang up on the west side of the river. Abraham Iredell, who had lived near Philadelphia and had been deputy surveyor in Northampton and Northumberland counties, Pa., settled in Parrtown, where he enjoyed half pay as a lieutenant of the Royal Guides and Pioneers, while serving as deputy surveyor of New Brunswick. Christopher Sauer, 3d., a printer of Germantown, began the publication of the *Royal Gazette* in Parrtown and was deputy post master of the Province in 1792, but returned to the States seven years later and died at Baltimore, Md., in July, 1799.[12]

It will be remembered that the principal corps in which Pennsylvanians enlisted were the Pennsylvania Loyalists, the Queen's Rangers, the Royal Guides and Pioneers, the New Jersey Volunteers, and the Philadelphia Light Dragoons. Most of the men of these organizations, except the last ones, had come to New Brunswick with Colonel Hewlett; and it remains for us to note the locations taken up by these regiments after their disbandment and some other items concerning them. The 1st and 3d battalions of the New Jersey Volunteers were among the Loyalist corps that preferred to remain at Parrtown and await new allotments of land, rather than ascend the river to the distant tracts at first assigned to them. Meantime, many of the men of the 3d battalion boarded schooners with their families for the winding and tedious voyage of nine or ten days to St. Ann's Point. As six inches of snow fell on November 2d, or about three weeks after their arrival, not a few were caught by the cold weather without other shelter than their tents. Some, to be sure, had managed to erect rude huts for their protection, or to be received into the cabins of earlier settlers along the river; but others took their tents into the depths of the forest and there set them up, where game and firewood abounded, and a poor kind of shelter was afforded by the thick woods. Nevertheless, the sufferings of these exiles were intense, and "the loyal Provincials' Burial Ground" at Salamanca was frequented by mourners, although the dead were not infrequently buried near the snow-banked tents of the living. When mild weather came the refugees made good use of their axes and saws in felling trees for the erection of log houses, which were

---

12 Raymond, "Early Days of Woodstock" in *The Dispatch of Woodstock, N. B.*, Dec. 5, 1906; *Sec. Rep., Archives of Ont.*, 1904, I, 198, 209, 237, 200; Sabine, *Loyalists of the Am. Rev.*, II, 323; Jack, *St. John: Prize Essay*, 65.

roofed with bark and lighted by small glass windows, while the fireplaces and chimneys were built of stone cemented with yellow clay. Among the houses erected at this time was that of Colonel Hewlett, who had lost his stores, tools, baggage, and other property to the value of £200 in the wreck of the *Martha*, one of the transports which had brought the Loyalist regiments to New Brunswick. Spring came none too soon in this Northern wilderness, for the people at Salamanca were already running short of provisions; but they were now able to supply themselves with pigeons, partridges, moose, fish, and edible roots, and to supplement their scanty supply of vegetable food by the discovery of large patches of beans, which had been planted by earlier inhabitants of the region, probably by the French.[13] A few members of the 3d battalion, as already noted on a preceding page, went from New York to Shelburne, N. S., and settled there.[14]

There was evidently a considerable number of the men of the 3d New Jersey Volunteers still at Parrtown as late as January 17, 1785, when Captain Samuel Ryerson of this battalion memorialized Governor Thomas Carleton in behalf of his waiting comrades for lands in the unoccupied parts of Prince William Parish and of a reserve of 4,000 acres below the Pokiok, on account as he affirmed of the distance and sterility of soil of Block No. 12, which they had originally drawn. However, Ryerson's petition was not then complied with, although both the memorialists and the men of the 1st New Jersey Volunteers, who had drawn Block No. 14, eventually obtained more convenient locations in the counties of York, Sunbury, and Queens. The 2d New Jersey Volunteers got settled without the disheartening delays experienced by its sister battalions, for it fell heir to one of the desirable tracts, namely, Block No. 2, which became the Parish of Kingsclear in 1786, and lies only about twenty miles above Fredericton. It contained 38,450 acres on the south side of the River St. John, and was granted under date of July 14, 1784, to Lieutenant Colonel Isaac Allen and 143 others of his battalion. Another grant of 14,050 acres on the headwaters of the Kennebecasis was made to Colonel Allen and 94 others in the same month and year. In 1799 the first mentioned grant to Allen and his men was canceled in chancery,

---

[13] Raymond, *The River St. John*, 548-550.
[14] *Rep. on the Am. Mss. in the Roy. Inst. of Gt. Brit.*, IV, 375, 376; Sabine, *Loyalists of the Am. Rev.*, II, 376. See *ante* p. 101.

and a new and much smaller grant at Mactaquac on the north bank of the St. John was assigned him and others.[15]

Two days after the Loyalist troops arrived at the mouth of the River St. John a small party of the Royal Guides and Pioneers came ashore, September 29, 1783, one day in advance of the general disembarkation. Presumably these men proceeded on their way up to St. Ann's Point on the 30th, for Colonel Hewlett wrote to Sir Guy Carleton at the time to that effect. They must therefore have shared in the hardships of the following winter. The rest of the Guides and Pioneers, except the company of Black Pioneers which embarked at New York in October, 1783, for Annapolis in Nova Scotia, remained at Parrtown. They drew Block No. 3 on the north side of St. John River above the Keswick, the mouth of which lay within their district. They took possession of their block in 1784, being joined later by other Loyalists; but it appears that their grant was not issued until November 7, 1787, and that it included what were known as Crock's Point and Burgoyne's Ferry. Some of the men of this corps also settled in Queensbury Parish along with the Queen's Rangers. Concerning the Black Pioneers, who had been attached to the corps of the Guides and Pioneers, Sir Guy Carleton's instructions to Brigadier General H. E. Fox were that Governor Parr should be asked to grant them a town lot and about twenty acres in the vicinage, in case they settled near a town like Shelburne, but that they be given a hundred acres in case they settled in the country as farmers.[16] The obvious intention of these instructions was that each member of the company should receive the amount of land mentioned.

On April 15, 1783, Major R. Armstrong, in the absence of Lieutenant Colonel John Graves Simcoe, commander of the Queen's Rangers, who had returned to England, authorized Colonel Edward Winslow to locate lands and obtain grants for the 575 persons then connected with the corps, of whom 305 were privates, sixty women, and seventy children. During the interval of five months that elapsed before the Rangers sailed with the other regiments for New Brunswick, their numerical strength seems to have declined

[15] Raymond, "Early Days of Woodstock" in *The Dispatch of Woodstock, N. B.,* Dec. 5, 19, 26, 1906; Ganong, *Monograph of Historic Sites in the Province of N. B.,* 340; Ganong, *Monograph of the Origins of the Settlements in N. B.,* 143, 341, 343.

[16] Raymond, *Winslow Papers,* 137; *Report on Am. Mss. in the Roy. Inst. of Gt. Brit.,* IV, 380, 49, 50, 420; Raymond, "Early Days of Woodstock" in *The Dispatch of Woodstock, N. B.,* Dec. 5, 1906; Ganong, *Monograph of the Origins of the Settlements in N. B.,* 112, 162; Ganong, *Monograph on Historic Sites in the Province of N. B.,* 343.

markedly. At Parrtown some of the Rangers drew lots and thus became grantees of the place; but the large majority, that is, more than two-thirds of those for whom Major Armstrong had requested grants, settled together on Block No. 5, or the Parish of Queensbury, on the north side of the River St. John. James Brown and sixty-six other Queen's Rangers received a grant of 17,674 acres in Queensbury as late as January 30, 1787.[17]

The corps of the Pennsylvania Loyalists, which numbered 171 men at the end of the year 1778, when it was sent with other troops to Pensacola to assist in the defense of West Florida against the Spaniards, had no more than sixty-eight men at the time of its return to New York in June, 1782. Between this date and the summer of 1784 nearly half of this number had scattered, for Thomas Knox, who took a census of the regiments on the River St. John during that summer, found but thirty-six men, fourteen women, eight children, and five servants belonging to the corps occupying their lands in Block No. 7, across the river from Woodstock. The presence of these settlers led to the establishment of the Parish of Northampton in 1786. On August 17th of the following year, William Burns and other Pennsylvania Loyalists received a grant of lands within the original block. The Parish of Southampton, which was also settled by members of the corps and their descendants, was not created until 1833. But not all of the men of the Pennsylvania Loyalists who came to New Brunswick settled in these parishes. The Reverend Doctor W. O. Raymond tells us that they were to be found at various places within the Province.[18]

---

[17] Siebert, "The Refugee Loyalists of Connecticut," in *Trans. Roy. Soc. Can.*, 1916, 85, 91; Rev. W. O. Raymond's Notes on Winslow's Muster Rolls (unpublished); Raymond, "Early Days of Woodstock" in *The Dispatch of Woodstock, N. B.*, Jan. 23, 1907; Raymond, *The River St. John*, 546; Ganong, *Monograph of Historic Sites in the Province of N. B.*, 341.

[18] Siebert "The Loyalists in West Florida and the Natchez District" in the *Miss. Valley Hist. Rev.*, II, March, 1916, 473, 481; Raymond, Notes on Winslow's Muster Rolls (unpublished); Raymond, *Winslow Papers*, 215, 216; Ganong, *Monograph of the Origins of the Settlements in N. B.*, 155, 173; Ganong, *Monograph of Historic Sites in the Province of N. B.*, 343; *Coll. N. B. Hist. Soc.*, No. 5 (1904), 209.

INDEX

www.ingramcontent.com/pod-product-compliance
Lightning Source LLC
Chambersburg PA
CBHW031130020426
42333CB00012B/314